MORE
CELTIC GREATS

MORE CELTIC GREATS

Hugh Keevins

SPORTSPRINT PUBLISHING
EDINBURGH

ISBN 0 85976 308 0

Phototypeset by Beecee Typesetting Services
Printed in Great Britain by Bell & Bain Ltd., Glasgow

Contents

Acknowledgements

I am greatly indebted to friends, associates and players, too numerous to mention individually, for the supply of many excellent illustrations.

H.K.

CHAPTER 1

Introduction

NOSTALGIA HAS NEVER BEEN SOMETHING IN which Celtic supporters have taken refuge when they find the present day not to their liking. The club has always believed itself to have what Billy McNeill called a 'fairytale aspect' and, from time to time, the wealth of memories to draw from is tapped on and the experience savoured, like any other memorable story that bears re-telling. Greatness with a club like Celtic is not restricted to that done while wearing green and white hoops either. Those who serve their country's national side well bring distrinction upon themselves and their club and Celtic have contributed players whose performances for Scotland, the Republic of Ireland and Northern Ireland over many decades exemplify that point.

Celtic's post-war successes, sporadic though they may have been in the beginning, were helped brought about by Bertie Peacock, an Ulsterman who took Northern Ireland into the latter stages of the World Cup in 1958 when, in times of more sophisticated media coverage, the achievement would have been the stuff of front page headlines and the obligatory civic reception. The unfailingly courteous Bertie, who has returned to live in Coleraine, also embodied Celtic's resolution to pick the best possible team without consideration for religious persuasion and with regard only to ability and a willingness to do well for the club and its supporters.

If Bertie Peacock knew little of Celtic and its traditions when he came over to Scotland, he developed such a strong attachment to them that, even when he was part of the Rest of the World eleven while his team struggled on the domestic front, the idea of leaving Celtic Park never entered his mind, though there were plenty of opportunities to go elsewhere. Such were the displays of Peacock in the company of Jock Stein and Bobby Evans, others who were not brought up to follow Celtic but would grow to cherish the club, the inspiration behind the side who would be synonomous with their greatest days, the late Sir Robert Kelly, would single them out for honourable mention at a potentially dishonourable Annual General Meeting.

The resolution before the meeting was that achievement for Celtic would only ever be in direct ratio to the number of Catholic players used in the first team.

Overcoming such suspicion and gaining the full respect of the supporters was managed by Peacock and, in the eyes of the more discerning, Willie Fernie. A Fifer of typically independent streak, Willie had literally walked miles and then travelled by train for hours to play for Celtic in the beginning then stood his ground by staying at home until he had convinced the management he was worthy of a game on a regular basis.

Fernie and Peacock would become members of the side who won Celtic their first League and Cup double for forty years, in 1954, and brought to the club one of its permanent treasures, the Coronation Cup, the year before. In 1957, there was recorded the result against Rangers in the League Cup final which remains a record for a national competition. Celtic's 7-1 demolition of their historic rivals has also been kept for posterity, remaining, decades after it happened, a conversation piece for those who were there and a suitable topic of discussion for others who were not even born when Willie Fernie scored the final goal and Bertie Peacock lifted the trophy as captain.

Fernie had majesterial control of the ball as well as the pace to use that quality to its best effect yet he had to leave the club and then return before he was fully appreciated by those who mistakenly believed him to be simply a greedy player.

Now a taxi driver in Glasgow, Willie can also reflect on the time spent as a coach at Celtic Park helping nurture the careers of so many who would attain greatness with the club, such as Danny McGrain and Tommy Burns. As an experienced player, though, Fernie, and Bertie Peacock brought on their younger contemporaries on the staff in the days when the most helpful lessons were those taught in the dressing room as opposed to the training ground.

Bertie Auld espoused the cause of Partick Thistle as someone who attached a deep significance to coming from Maryhill but his relationship with Celtic, leading at one time to a trial separation, became the abiding love of his life. Encouraged by his father to sign for Jimmy McGrory rather than the then Partick Thistle manager, Davie Meiklejohn, the impetuosity of youth would sometimes get the better of Bertie and convinced Bob Kelly that, temperamentally speaking, he was a hopeless case. On the night that Jock Stein's Dunfermline were beating Celtic in the replay of the Scottish Cup final of 1961, Bertie was busily scoring three goals in a reserve match and preparing to sign for Birmingham City the following day.

A triumphal homecoming would be years away and, in the interim, it would befall those who were known as the 'Kelly Kids' to negotiate Celtic's path through difficult times. Pat Crerand would, in any era, have been considered an outstanding performer for Celtic. It would be his misfortune, however, to serve the club at a time when he lacked the quality of players around him to make the best of his exceptional passing ability, creativity and commitment to the team for whom he still holds the deepest affection to this day.

Crerand's time with Celtic would be punctuated by controversy, on and off the park, but he was of Irish descent and came from the Gorbals. To have expected anything like a quiet life would have been unreasonable. There would have to be a profound sense of what might have been over Crerand. Had he been able to forebear what was going on about him for a little while longer, until Jock Stein assumed his rightful place as manager at Celtic Park, Pat's status could have gone close to the state of deification in the minds of the supporters.

It was indicative of the way Stein's mind worked that before he had taken over control diplomatic overtures were made to Bertie Auld in Birmingham over the possibility of a return to the East End of Glasgow as part of the managers vision of the ideal Celtic. The response, which came the night before an F.A. Cup tie against West Ham measured the depth of Bertie's feeling for, and anguish over the separation from, Celtic Park.

'D'ye want me to come up tonight?' was the reply. Celtic needed an experienced head to guide the greatest crop of players it has ever been the club's good fortune to have assembled under one roof at the same time. It is the case, in fact, that there are now men in their twenties who are legally registered as having their Christian names separated from their family name by Simpson, Craig, Gemmell, Murdoch, McNeill, Clark, Johnstone, Wallace, Chalmers, Auld and Lennox. It was the team forever recalled only by their collective title, the Lisbon Lions.

Contained within Celtic's European Cup-winning side of 1967 are figures who elevated a Saturday afternoon out at the football to never before imagined heights of pleasure and wonderment. Tommy Gemmell was a full back only in that he wore a number three on his shorts. He was larger than life and twice as cheeky, the personification of what it was thought a Celtic player should be like for the way in which he insisted on playing the game as if it were a form of entertainment.

To say Tommy reveled in the adulation would be to achieve one hundred per cent accuracy. Blessed with the boundless energy that was necessary to do the running he did, and possessed by a ferocious shot, Tommy was part of a unit who believed themselves to be unbeatable and could truthfully have been said to have lifted the game to the level of an art form. When Tommy left for Nottingham Forest, he believed himself to have signed away a part of his life with the tranfer agreement yet he also knows there are some who think of him only as Gemmell of Celtic, scorer of one of the goals that beat Inter Milan in Lisbon and accessory to countless others.

In the business of scoring for Celtic, though, the post-war record is held by someone who made his birthplace of Saltcoats, on the Ayrshire coast, famous for something other than buckets and spades, Bobby Lennox. Bobby played throughout his career with a sunny disposition and even survived a broken leg to remain an integral part of Celtic's plans until into his mid thirties and yet, prior to Jock Stein's arrival, he could have been sold for a pittance to Falkirk and a classic case of the one who got away might have been able to be put against Celtic's name.

As if his accomplishment in helping win nine League Championship titles in a row, as well as the European Cup, was not enough, Bobby also enjoyed a glorious Indian Summer with Celtic. Allowed to go to America for what appeared to be his swansong, Lennox was re-signed by Billy McNeill when he succeeded Jock Stein and then picked up the threads of his career in typically stunning fashion, going out on the fittingly high note of a winning appearance in the Scottish Cup final of 1980, against Rangers.

With him on the field that day was Tommy Burns, for whom each game for Celtic was made to look exactly what it was, the fulfilment of a lifetime's ambition. Tommy was born within sight of Celtic Park and educated at St. Mary's school in the Calton, where the club had been brought into being by a Marist Brother, Walfrid, in the previous century. He was, therefore, imbued with the Celtic spirit and felt a close bond with all aspects of the club, its tradition and supporters. The affection was reciprocated by the fans and this was demonstrated twice, once on the occasion of his testimonial match, against Liverpool, and again when, in December, 1989, an illustrious career, rich in League and Cup medals, came to an end when there was an emotional parting of the ways during a friendly match against Ajax.

There are those, like Burns, who are held in such high regard they are part of the club's fabric. Charlie Nicholas' first time with Celtic saw him play in only 109 matches but in that time he attained a cult following that put him above others who had spent the equivalent of a lifetime wearing green and white. It would also be fair to say there were those who pined for Charlie's return from the moment he left, in June, 1983, until he came back, in July, 1990. Absence's effect on the hearts of the Celtic supporters had been visibly demonstrated when, during a match between their club and Aberdeen at Celtic Park, Charlie, while in the act of being substituted by the latter, had received a standing ovation from the home crowd and responded by clapping those with whom he had an undeniable affinity.

The script, as Charlie acknowledges, could not have been better written so far as his return is concerned if he had been given pen and paper himself. Within these pages, in fact, Nicholas will tell how hard he found the job of motivating himself to play against Celtic, even though he had to be resolutely professional and, with his last kick of the ball as an Aberdeen player, scored one of the goals in the penalty decider wich cost Celtic the Scottish Cup and, along with it, a place in Europe.

It was a penalty kick decider, during the World Cup finals in Italy, which brought Pat Bonner to the attention of a worldwide audience and encouraged the coach of Barcelona, Johan Cruyff, to consider asking Celtic to name their price for the Republic of Ireland internationalist who has now shown himself to be at the peak of his career. Bonner's story, though, began in the small Donegal fishing village of Burton Port. One of seven children, Pat had never seen Celtic play but was fully conversant on the affairs of the club because of a neighbour whose hall was made noticeable because of a portrait of the

Lisbon Lions. Recommended to Sean Fallon during his time as assistant manager, Packy ultimately became Jock Stein's last ever signing for the club, thereby maintaining the club's historic links with Ireland. When the time came for the teenager to leave his family and move to Glasgow, the state of nervous anxiety was such Pat had to be confined to bed for the twenty four hours befoe his departure and can clearly remember breaking down and crying as the bus taking him on the first leg of his journey drove past the spot where he would fish in the summer in the compnay of his father, now passed away, and his twin brother, Denis.

The distraught youngster, though, made a pact with himself in his moment of grief. Pat swore not to return to Ireland until he had made his name as Bonner of Celtic. There would be few, least of all the Rumanian, Timote, who would deny that he has fully accomplished his aim in life.

His only regret in life now is that his father, Andrew, was not spared long enough to see what he has been able to achieve at Celtic Park and for the national side, whose previous manager, Eoin Hand, was reluctant to consider Packy because he played for a Scottish club.

Packy is now the longest serving player with the club and fully entitled to take his place among the best ever to have adorned their jersey. From one Irishman, Bertie Peacock, to another, Packy Bonner, the story spans forty years of achievement, good times and bad. Each player here gave generously of his time and Tommy Gemmell lived up to his image by selling the author an insurance policy before he left! All of them have an interesting story to tell of how their lives were, to one degree or another, shaped by association with the club that is the repository for those who believe football should be played in a thrilling, entertaining and memorable way, Celtic.

CHAPTER 2

Willie Fernie

THERE ARE THOSE PLAYERS WHOSE GENERAL lack of control was best summed up by a contemporary of Willie Fernie's, who said that the species was instantly identifiable because they would have needed a harpoon gun to kill the ball. For all that Fernie had a mastery of the ball, however, he spent his entire career being viewed with suspicion, both by the spectating public and the media. As a player, he had been part of a Celtic side who had won a league and cup double in 1954 after earlier bringing historical distinction to the club by helping to win the Coronation Cup (in the midst of triumph at Hampden, Charlie Tully told him: 'If you had a left foot, we would have had the game won at half time!') There are twenty-two Celtic players who have gained immortality during the reign of Queen Elizabeth II, half of them made up the European Cup-winning side of 1967, the others were Celtic's League Cup-winning team from ten years earlier. Fernie was the player who got the goal in the last minute of the match against Rangers which saw Celtic win 7-1 and create the highest score yet recorded in a domestic cup final as well as a memory that does not diminish with the passing of time, even for those supporters who were not born when the club was given something for posterity. Before and after the completion of those achievements, Fernie had also taken part in two World Cup finals for Scotland, and yet at club and international level he was accused of being a selfish player who nullified his undoubted grace, artistry, speed and strength by giving the impression that he would only part with the ball if it were absolutely necessary before losing possession to the other side.

When the player became a manager, he took with him to Kilmarnock his philosophy of how the game should be played in order to derive maximum satisfaction and brought together a team that was the envy of others for the entertainment they produced yet did not encourage anybody else to copy what they did. The reason for that was simple: what Willie Fernie peddled was too refined for those with the more basic need of wanting to stay in the Premier Divison.

Partly for refusing to take the pragmatic view that it was better not to buck the system, Willie Fernie was sacked while having the most admired team in the league. So, in 1976, there came to an end a career that could have been said to have been based entirely on something that was said to Willie by Dan Murphy, the scout responsible for bringing the then teenager from Fife to Celtic Park in 1948.

'Dan's first words of advice to me were, ''Never pass the ball unless it is to your team's advantage.'' It was a lesson I tried to absorb and put into practice throughout my career, but retaining possession and never getting rid of the ball just to put my burden on to someone else's shoulders was what earned me the reputation of being a greedy player and ensured the crowds could never make up their mind about me.'

What was indisputable, however, was that the combination of grace and strength possessed by the player discovered by Dan Murphy and Jimmy McGrory when Willie was playing for Leslie Hearts in the Fife Secondary Juvenile League. From the tender age of fourteen, Willie had done the physically demanding manual labour of an adult on a farm for nine hours a day and built up considerable body strength (one of his first mentions in a newspaper match report, he recalls, wrote of the 'barrel chested Fernie'). The family's preoccupation with training greyhounds, which they raced all over the country, may also have helped develop the fleetness of foot which, allied to a long stride, enabled him to drift past opponents with ease. McGrory and Murphy had seen enough in one Juvenile cup final against Vale Emmett, in any case, to decide he should become Celtic's property. Arriving at the Fernie household after the game, though, they discovered the house empty.

'The neighbours had seen them come and go and that was what annoyed me more than anything, the fact that I had missed the chance to meet the legendary Jimmy McGrory. Remember, I hadn't had the opportunity to do much other than read about football. I was eighteen before I went to see my first senior match, when I was taken to watch East Fife play Motherwell, and, ironically, the only other famous name I had ever met was Scot Symon (later to become Rangers manager), who tried to get me to go to Bayview as a player. Luckily, Mr McGrory and Dan Murphy came back to see the Cup final replay that had been necessary but, of all things, I had to go off with a broken jaw. What impressed me was that the manager still came back to the house and reassure me of Celtic's interest and so I agreed to sign for the club.

'The journey from the village of Kinglassie, which was where I stayed, to Glasgow took three hours by train in those days and when I made the return trip there was also a five-mile walk from Thornton, where I left the train, back home again. That never bothered me so much as not getting a regular game at Celtic Park. I had never thought of a career in football in the first place so all I wanted to do was enjoy myself by playing every week and if I couldn't manage that, then I didn't see any point in staying on. I told Celtic as much and I was allowed, therefore, to play with Kinglassie Colliery instead of staying in Glasgow. Then, I received a telegram telling me it was time to return to the club and I made my debut for Celtic's first team against St Mirren at Paisley.'

What Fernie could have done with then, in fact, was the guidance of a more experienced man, the kind of job he would

Willie Fernie — Left the farm and off to Celtic Park.

do for Celtic three decades later when he became the mentor responsible for shaping the early careers of everyone from Danny McGrain and Kenny Dalglish to Tommy Burns.

'We trained behind the goals at Celtic Park in the fifties and there was, I believe, one ball for 26 players to share. Football boots were worn on a Saturday afternoon and not put on again until the following weekend because all training was done in sandshoes. That was just the way it was then and we accepted that as much as the fact that the manager was rarely seen at training. Any talking that was done about the game was carried on over the lunch dishes at Ferrari's Restaurant in Glasgow, where the players were given a meal each day on the club. Big Jock (Stein) would lead the tactical discussion, using salt and pepper cellars, sugar bowls and sauce bottles as his players. The conversation would only be brought to a close when somebody would whisper "Big Bob's coming" and a hush would descend.'

'Big Bob' was Celtic's benignly autocratic chairman, Robert Kelly. Each player at Celtic Park was looked upon as a son by him and he inspired in them a respectfulness that was in keeping with the kind of relationship a father would have with his children. It was no secret, either, that team selection was taken out of managerial hands at Celtic Park in those days and moved into the boardroom or that autocracy could extend into the dressing room, where Kelly was known to go to exhort the players to ever greater heights. Such was his single-minded devotion to Celtic, Kelly did not believe that there existed such a thing as a team that was superior to his boys, and pre-match encouragement would take a fevered, but non-tactical aspect.

'You are a better team than they are. Just go out, enjoy yourselves and prove that,' he would tell the players.

The selection process could sometimes take on a mysterious dimension, though, and Willie remembers playing in a two-legged League Cup tie against Rangers which betrayed what was going on. The first leg was won 4-0 but in the return match, four days later, Fernie was left out for no reason other than to make space for an untried youngster, Matt McVittie, and with the inevitable consequences. Rangers won 4-1. It took until 1951, by which time he had moved to Glasgow, for Willie to become an established member of the first team at Celtic Park. His absorption into West of Scotland culture did not extend to making regular appearances at Celtic Supporters' functions, unlike the more naturally gregarious types, like Charlie Tully, and that East of Scotland reserve as well as a need for a genuinely private life may have helped create distance between Fernie and those on the terracing who would develop an ambivalent attitude towards him. That he had embraced the club and its traditions and wanted to do the best he could for them was not in any doubt, however.

Celtic's journey through the fifties was an erratic one: the

Willie Fernie faces up to the camera.

Scottish Cup win in 1951 was followed by elimination at the first-round stage the year afterwards, while the Coronation Cup was taken by a side whose primary attraction for the organisers of the event was not so much the threat they posed to the other teams but the club's capacity for drawing huge crowds. The double, won in 1954, was the club's first for forty years, Fernie's dribble and cross for Fallon having brought the Scottish Cup back to Celtic Park in the process. The decade, though, did contain the result that had acted as a source of provocation to Rangers' supporters since Celtic won the League Cup at Hampden in a way that had become folklore.

'It was a day when all eleven players did well and by going about their work in the studied way in which the game was meant to be played. Even Rangers contributed to the match as a spectacle by refusing to do anything underhand and playing the games in the true spirit. That was still the case when the score was getting to a serious stage for them, a barely credible one for Celtic.

'I would say that Rangers' goal, in fact, scored by Billy Simpson, might even have been the best of the eight in the match. The attitude of the Celtic players, though, was "let's keep trying to get more goals" which explains why we were able to be awarded a penalty in the final minute. I took the kick but I was not what could have been called a penalty expert. Billy McPhail had scored a hat-trick and really ought to have gone for four goals in a domestic final, something which had never been done before, but he gave the ball to me and it was typical of the kind of day we were having that I put the ball past my fellow Fifer, George Niven, with ease. If we had won the cup by only one goal it would still have been a marvellous achievement, because we were not expected to win. However, I don't recall being aware of any outstanding significance where the 7-1 result was concerned. I can't even remember where the players went to celebrate afterwards.'

The remainder of that evening would have been a blur for tens of thousands of others who had been at Hampden as well. Those hangovers would pass with varying degrees of speed but the lavish win over Rangers led, perversely, to an eight-year-long period of abject failure for Celtic and one that Willie Fernie would be able to see from various angles, starting with a look back at Celtic's main door. A year after the League Cup final, he asked for a transfer and was sold to Middlesbrough, then in England's Second Division, for £16,000.

'By then I had been in the professional game for ten years but with nothing to show for my efforts. Also, I had married Audrey, who had been secretary to Jimmy McGrory for eight of those years. In short, I went from Celtic because I wanted to get some kind of money behind me, not through any premonition of what was to come or out of boredom with my surroundings after that length of time.

The majesterial control of Fernie.

'The truth of that statement is easily verified because I came back to Celtic two years later in spite of the fact that I was not getting a signing-on fee. As well as that, I accepted a weekly wage that was less than some others of the time were getting and I was a Scottish internationalist. In fairness, though, I did get help from the club to buy the house I still live in to this day with Audrey and our family.'

During the years at Middlesbrough, Willie came into contact with a young centre forward whose ability was as unquestionable as his manner was dubious. His name was Brian Clough. To say that Fernie and Clough did not see eye to eye was a gross understatement and Willie's conversation can be peppered with an assortment of adjectives to describe someone with whom the entire Middlesbrough team, with one notable exception, would fall out.

'In my first game for the club, Clough knocked me out of the way to score an easy goal. That was the kind of striker he was and with an average of forty goals in each of the seasons I was at Ayresome Park Brian had a record that could not be criticised, unlike his manners. There was no doubt that Clough and the team's goalkeeper, Peter Taylor, would pick the team in the manager's office each Saturday afternoon. Taylor, of course, eventually formed a successful partnership in management with Brian and I know where they had their grounding in the business! The one piece of credit that would have to be given to Brian Clough is that his teams have always played the game as I believe it should be played. His players are never regimented but allowed to express themselves freely and it is impossible to ignore Brian's record on the domestic front and in Europe, having won the Champions Cup in successive seasons with Nottingham Forest.

'As a player, though, Brian's personality was so abrasive that when the manager, Bob Dennison, decided he should be made team captain at Middlesbrough there was a full-scale revolt. Every player on the staff, with the obvious exception of Peter Taylor, was opposed to the idea and 28 of us filed into the boardroom to put our objections on record. Clough sat through that meeting, too, unmoved by the fact that he had just one friend in the world so far as the dressing room was concerned.'

Fernie and Clough had taken an instant dislike to each other. Clough's arrogance was the stuff of legend in Middlesbrough, where he had grown up and become a hero because of his goalscoring exploits. Celebrity would cause the opinionated young man to hold up team buses and trains while he made a dramatic, if belated, entrance, wearing his football boots round his neck. The cloth cap that Clough wore would be taken off and thrown with a flourish at his dressing-room peg each morning. It was not the kind of theatrical behaviour ever likely to endear him to a man from the mining community of the East of Scotland where they had a variety of unpleasant names for people who behaved like that. Such was the viciousness of Clough's tongue when he felt the ball was not being passed to him often, or correctly, enough that he had reduced one of his team-mates to a state of nervous anxiety far worse than any opposing team could have done. Not surprisingly, then, there was another supposed colleague who took gleeful delight in bringing one morning training session to an abrupt halt by kicking Clough so badly he had to be taken away for treatment. The relationship between Fernie and Clough was doomed from the start. Angry words would be exchanged if Willie chose to beat another defender rather than pass to him, giving rise to the latter calling his team-mate 'My ball Fernie' in his weekly newspaper column.

That tactic and the local hero's habit of demonstrating disgust whenever a move broke down at Willie's feet managed to turn a section of the support at Ayresome Park against the former Celtic player.

'Years later, when I was manager of Kilmarnock, we were drawn against Nottingham Forest in the Anglo-Scottish Cup and I made a point of going to look for Clough at the team's hotel on the outskirts of Glasgow because I was sure he had avoided me when we played the first leg at the City Ground. When I found him, there he was with his feet up on a table in the lounge, wearing no shoes or socks. When I approached, Brian could not have been nicer and shocked me by standing up in front of everyone and saying that all the things I had said about him when he was younger were absolutely true. Not for the first time, Cloughie left me speechless!'

English football, the aggravation of having to keep some people company notwithstanding, had been a pleasurable experience for Willie, whose skills were more widely appreciated. Settling down in the North East of England was not so easily done, though, and Willie was eventually returned to a Celtic side who needed all the help they could get at that time.

'My job was to help the club back on its feet and I am happy that I made a contribution in that direction. I'll always remember running out at Love Street for my return appearance and schoolboys coming over the boundary walls to welcome me back. The hairs on the back of my head stood on end and there was a genuine feeling of homecoming. Had we won the Scottish Cup final against Dunfermline at the end of that season, I think I would have gone on to finish my playing career with Celtic but the disappointment of losing was so great for everybody at the club that I found myself on my way again, this time to St Mirren.

'We should have beaten Dunfermline, too. There were certainly enough chances to do so in the first game while the replay went down in Scottish Cup history as ''Connaghan's Final'', because of the superb display by Dunfermline's goalkeeper, Eddie Connaghan, I felt Celtic threw away the game yet again, both by missing more opportunities ourselves and by making defensive errors that cost us a trophy which could have eased a considerable burden on the club.'

The oppressive weight on Celtic's shoulders would soon be aided by Fernie himself. His move to St Mirren eventually saw Willie play against Celtic in the semi-final of the Scottish Cup at Ibrox, the following season. As well as scoring the opening goal for the Paisley club, Fernie orchestrated St Mirren's domination of the game, and the cries of 'traitor' he can recall as he came off the park could, while hurtful, have been taken as confirmation of his supreme influence over the outcome. Willie's time at Love Street was short-lived, in any case, and there was a gradual realisation on his part that his days in the

Fernie the coach — 'The game is a form of entertainment'.

game as a player were coming to an end. A nondescript time in Ireland was followed by a short stay at Alloa before Willie decided it was better to bow to the inevitable. The job he found working as a car salesman with the firm owned by the two men who now run Clydebank F.C., Jack and Charles Steedman, might have been thought timely since they then owned East Stirling. However, no offer of additional employment on the coaching side was forthcoming and Willie Fernie's professional association with the game might have drawn to a premature close had it not been for Jock Stein bringing him back to Celtic in 1967.

'The European Cup had just been won by the club but they also had a remarkable crop of youngsters like Kenny Dalglish, Danny McGrain, Lou Macari, George Connelly and Davie Hay. I can remember taking them to Ibrox once when they beat a far more experienced Rangers side 6-0 in a reserve game.

'It was then I started to put into practice all the ideas I had nurtured on how to coach, though another one was hastily formed out of necessity. There were so many players on the books at Celtic Park then that space was at a premium and the young players were often left to train in a confined space behind one goal. One day, I decided to take them out into the car park in front of the main door and devised a game that had no goals. The object of the exercise was to make the players think about retaining possession and making passes, thereby improving their general awareness of what was going on around them.'

When that group had, one by one, graduated to the first team under Stein, there were others coming along, such as Tommy Burns, who would also have cause to be grateful to WIllie for the work he put in on their development and the recommendations he would make to Sean Fallon and Jock Stein over who should be signed by the club. Burns, for instance, was short, bespectacled and thought to have made his entry into Celtic Park under false pretences until Fernie's persistence paid off in convincing the management that it was better to grab the youngster before somebody else did and made Celtic look foolish. After six years of fulfilling that type of role, Willie became restless because of his lack of a position carrying greater authority and consequently took over the job as manager of Kilmarnock.

'At first, though, I couldn't see why a new man was required. The team had a lowly position in the old-style Second Division, but after looking at the players in one game I couldn't find much fault with them. All they lacked was someone to help them believe in themselves. Some time later, I attended an S.F.A. coaching course and had my views on the game questioned by another club manager who wanted to know why I didn't agree that it was fundamental to approach every game with the intention of making sure that, first and foremost, it was not lost.

'My answer was that I took the game to be a form of

entertainment. For all that happened to me later on, I still believe I was correct in what I said. The Premier Division today is made up of 360 matches a season, of which one third, on average, end up as draws. That is not good enough for the paying public, to my way of thinking. It is too simple to say I became a martyr for the cause of attacking football, though. In the end it was a combination of certain players and directors who got me the sack at Rugby Park.'

Kilmarnock were twice promoted and once relegated during Willie's time as manager. At the beginning of his final season with the club, the manager asked in the customary manner what size of bonus payment the players would receive for each point gained. No answer was forthcoming and resentment began to simmer in the dressing room. Ultimately, Willie was brought before the board and told that he would be removed unless four points were forthcoming from the team's next two matches. Both games were lost and there was a distinct feeling that some players had given up trying as hard as they might for their idealistic manager.

'If I had my time over again, I wouldn't do things any differently, It took me a long while, though, to get over what happened to me at Kilmarnock. I was on the dole for a while, drawing £42 a week, before I decided it was time to look for a job away from football.'

Willie Fernie now drives a taxi in Glasgow and enjoys a better lifestyle as a result than he did while involved in football. It is not uncommon for him, either, to look in the rear-view mirror while conducting conversations with customers who deem it an honour to be chauffeured by one whose reputation has grown over the intervening years. Hindsight being what it is, Willie gets greater respect now than he did during his playing days.

The Celtic influence is still strong in the Fernie household, too. His son, Andrew, is a season ticket holder at Celtic Park and a devout follower of the team wherever they are playing. On a Saturday afternoon, though, the man who did so much for the club in the fifties gets his information on Celtic's progress from the radio he keeps in his driver's cabin. If Celtic are losing, the radio is quickly switched off, his listening habits being as arbitrary as the judgement of those who, once upon a time, were never fully convinced of his merit as a player, but who, given cause for sober reflection, might now think differently.

Willie Fernie *International Appearances*

1954

May	Finland (a)	2-1
June	Austria (a)	0-1
June	Uruguay (a)	0-7
October	Wales (a)	1-0
November	Northern Ireland (h)	2-2

1956

November	Yugoslavia (h)	2-0

1957

April	England (a)	1-2
November	Switzerland (h)	3-2
November	Wales (h)	1-1

1958

June	Paraguay (a)	1-2

CHAPTER 3

Pat Crerand

PAT CRERAND AND BILLY McNEILL WALKED through the front door of Celtic Park on the same day in 1957 and, over the years that followed, accompanied each other on a hard road through years of disappointment with the team for which they shared an identical, passionate commitment. If McNeill's journey eventually took him to a hallowed place in the club's history as a player whose record of achievement saw him lead Celtic to nine successive league championships as well as becoming the first Briton to get his hands on the European Cup, Crerand would ultimately leave Glasgow without anything to show for his equally instinting effort on the team's behalf. To this day, that remains a source of deep frustration for Pat and one that would be shared by those who could appreciate the quality he brought to a side that was enriched by his presence as a forceful right half. It is typical of the depth of feeling he retains for Celtic, though, that he counts among his most cherished memories the days on which he was able to participate in the side's subsequent triumphs as a supporter whenever his commitments with Manchester United allowed. First and foremost, Pat Crerand was, and still is, a Celtic supporter.

Where Pat was born and brought up, at Crown Street in the Gorbals, everybody supported Celtic and looked upon the club as an expression of their identity, the community being largely of Irish extraction. Born shortly before the outbreak of the Second World War, the second oldest of a family of four, Pat was two years old when, on the night of March 12, 1941, his father, fire-watching in John Brown's shipyard in Clydebank, was killed during the blitz. The following day the youngest of the Crerand family, Pat's sister Mary, was born.

A widowed mother, left with four young children to bring up in a room and kitchen during a time of rationing, struggled heroically to see her family never went without while her children found themselves shaped by their circumstances and surroundings.

It was a rough time but it taught me to fend for myself. Everybody around about us was in the same position, being skint, and I can remember getting up at the crack of dawn to deliver milk in order to bring in what I could. Once that was done, I would take myself off to the playground of my primary school, St. Luke's, for half past seven. That was when the first football match of the day would take place. The game was the only thing we had available to us by way of recreation. There was no television to distract us and when we weren't playing, and being chased by the police for having a game in places where we shouldn't have been, there was only one other thing that introduced an element of community and that was following Celtic.

'Apart from that I don't recall much about the early days, apart from all of us kids sleeping in one room while my mother slept in the kitchen. The first thing you learned, though, was that there were two types of people in the world — Catholics and Protestants. You were either one or the other because there was no such thing as a neutral. The Crerands belonged to the former, being one of many Irish families who came to Scotland and settled in the Gorbals. There, if somebody didn't like you, he hit you and you hit him back again straight away, whether he was bigger or not. If you didn't, and the word was spread around, you were branded a cissy and then everybody in the neighbourhood had a belt at you.

Pat Crerand in the colours he dreamed of wearing.

'It was also the days of the razor gangs and I will never forget what happened to the old, Polish cobbler who had a shop in our street. His business was suddenly closed down for weeks and when I saw him again he had a scar which ran from his right ear to the side of his mouth. What kept me on the straight and narrow was being blessed with the mother I had. I was in bed by 6.30 every night until I was nine years old and not allowed to stay out beyond 9.30 until I was seventeen years of age.

It was Pat's mother who eventually offered the piece of advice which took him from being a fanatical Celtic supporter to a place on the club's register of players. For all that he had been picked for Glasgow's schoolboy side, graduation to the national team never did follow and the promising young player's potential was in danger of failing to be realised.

'Celtic were playing at home, against East Fife, and I was getting ready to go to the game until a man called Mick McGinlay came to our door. Mick ran a team in the Gorbals called Rancel, the name being proof that while there had been religious differences in the community, these were not allowed to be permanently divisive. He wanted me to play for the team that afternoon but I would still have been out the door and on my way to the tram for Celtic Park had my mother not put her foot down, pointing out that the match was not an important one in the first place and that I was being given a chance by someone who had been good enough to think about me. I was only with the team a short while when I was asked to play for the now defunct Duntocher Hibs, a junior team from the fringes of Clydebank.

The young Pat made an immediate impression at that grade and senior clubs, most notably Manchester City, would have enticed him away had it not been for Duntocher's manager, Jimmy McLean, appreciating that there was only one club who could have captured the attention of the teenager and they were situated much nearer to the Crerand household than Maine Road. It was after a match against Ashfield that Celtic's chief scout made his approach.

'Jimmy McLean stopped me coming off the pitch. He kept laughing and saying, "You're going to like this." We went into a small side room where he introduced me to a complete stranger, Teddy Swift. I can remember Teddy's exact words, "How would you like to join Celtic?" Seven words, seventh heaven. Joining Celtic meant I was also able to give up my job as an apprentice welder in Fairfield's shipyard, which was within walking distance of Rangers' ground in Govan. I wasn't in the slightest bit sorry about that because the atmosphere in the yard in those days could be intimidating due to the intensity of feeling over the Old Firm. I was a target for abuse from the Rangers supporters because, in their eyes, Duntocher Hibs represented a junior version of Celtic. In the yard, as in the Gorbals, I had to be ready to defend myself.

'There were three of us who walked nervously through the front door at Celtic Park, myself, big Billy and a lad called Andy Murphy. To the supporters who are too young to remember how it was in the late fifties, or weren't even born by then, those were trying times to be a Celtic man. Rangers were the dominant force in the land, and getting a corner kick could be a big thrill for Celtic. The team maintained its support because following Celtic was something you were born into, and as in the most caring of families, the more the team struggled, the closer you stood by them to offer help.

'The basic trouble, as I soon discovered once on the inside, was that the club had fallen into a disorganised state. There were strong influences on the young players, like Jock Stein, Charlie Tully and Bertie Peacock, but while the directors had goodness in their hearts and a deep-rooted love of the club, they had little else to offer. It was a tragedy that Jock was not able to exert his authority at that time. He was like a god to me and the others yet he was never too busy to help put us at ease. Bertie Peacock was not only an influential driving force on the park but he also made time to share his knowledge of the game with the younger element. I would always consider it my good fortune, too, that I played beside Charlie Tully during my first year in Celtic's reserve side. He was Irish and he was a character, which meant that he suited me down to the ground because I had also idolised him from the terracing as well.'

Enthusiasm was difficult to maintain, however, under the prevailing circumstances and, once into the first team on a regular basis, frustration could often manifest itself in Pat's case through disciplinary problems on the field. In the first eight games of the season in which Pat graduated from the reserve side, for example, Celtic used a total of 21 players. His first Old Firm game, won 3-2 at Ibrox, was Celtic's first victory over their historic rivals in eight, successive attempts. Pat, though, performed with such distinction he became a member of Scotland's full international side before the Scottish Cup final in 1961, against Dunfermline, which began to instil in him the feeling, however regrettable, that Celtic were going nowhere. To lose to Dunfermline was bad enough but to go down, after a replay to a side managed by Jock Stein, who had left Celtic 13 months earlier, was more than Pat could reasonably withstand and he left the pitch at Hampden crying tears of anger.

'I knew that night any player could only have a limited future with an unsuccessful club. The way Celtic were going then started to have an effect on my game and my personality. A week before the following season was due to begin, I was sent off in a five-a-side tournament that was staged at Falkirk's Brockville Park, though I will always protest my total innocence. The referee that day was Bobby Davidson and the atmosphere might have been most accurately described as hostile in a town where Celtic men were in short supply. The rules of the abbreviated game were that it was illegal to pass the ball backwards inside your own half of the field. When an opposing player took a throw in and directed the ball backwards, I claimed a foul but the referee would have none of it. If I had sworn at Mr Davidson, I would have been the first to say I deserved all that I got but all I did, using perfectly reasonable language, was plead for the proper observance of the rules. When the referee paid no attention, I kept on at him and he responded by deciding to send me off. To add insult to injury, I was then suspended for a month by the S.F.A.'

The game's governing body had not endeared itself to Pat as a result of an earlier dismissal while wearing a Scotland jersey. During a 4-0 defeat from Czechoslovakia in Bratislava, Scotland had been reduced to ten men when Pat punched an opponent, Kvasnak, and without asking for any mitigation circumstances to be taken into consideration.

'It was a World cup qualifying tie and therefore a tough and aggressive game for both sides. Kvasnak was a good player but he kept kicking me and after I had tackled him strongly he lost his temper and punched me. Reverting to my upbringing in the Gorbals, I belted him back and the referee sent off the pair of us.

'The incident happened at the far end of the ground, which meant it was a long walk back to the dressing room. As we paced it out in front of a highly excitable crowd, the thought occured to me that Kvasnak, who didn't look too pleased with me, might attempt a re-match in the tunnel. He was well over six feet tall, and realising that he might be able to call upon some of his fellow countrymen to help him vent his anger, I made up my mind to break into a sharp sprint the moment the tunnel came into sight. I might have come from the Gorbals, but I wasn't daft! However, he must have read messages into the look on my face as well, because as we turned off the track he broke into a run and didn't stop until he was on the safe side of the dressing-room door.'

If there was a funny side to the incident, it escaped the S.F.A., who took the unprecedented step of suspending Pat at club level for a period of seven days. Celtic's chairman, Bob Kelly, a man who was always intolerant of players from his club being associated with misbehavior on the field, also fined Pat £75, which was more than half the amount he was receiving in wages per month at that time, and added a suspension of his own.

'Bob Kelly would rather have had a Celtic player turn the other cheek than become involved in anything he considered to be too physical on the park and, indirectly, it was that attitude which eventually took me away from the club. Matters came to a head between Celtic and me on New Year's Day, 1963, at Ibrox. Our inside forwards that day were Charlie Gallagher and Bobby Murdoch, who was then a youngster and not as powerful as he would later become. The two of them were being brushed aside by Rangers players like Harold Davis and

Bobby Shearer, who were the kind not likely to take suspects, never mind prisoners. During the half-time discussion, I said that, on the brick-hard conditions, we should have been playing the ball to the feet of our own men and putting their big fellas under greater pressure that way.

'Sean Fallon disagreed with me and said the best idea was to get the ball up the park from the back as quickly as possible and charge on. We were a goal down already, though, and since that had come about after the ball had taken a deflection off me, there was an even harder edge to my temper. I told Sean exactly how much I disagreed with his tactical approach and words were exchanged at such a rate I found myself eventually taking off my jersey and refusing to go out for the second half. The dressing room had gone very quiet by then as I announced that Celtic could find somebody else to take my place, which was an impossibility, of course, since this was in the days before substitutes were permitted. Now, Sean Fallon was, still is and always will be a good friend of mine and our relationship was not damaged in any way by that row but Celtic went on to lose the game 4-0 and because of what I said I never played for the team again. In fact, two weeks later, I was sold to Manchester United.'

In the meantime, the outcry from supporters who wrote letters to Pat begging him not to go was ignored by Celtic's management, who, led by Bob Kelly, would never brook dissent from a player.

'If you argued with the chairman, you were finished, no matter who you were. The irony for me was that the release of all my pent-up frustration should occur during an Old Firm derby. Like any other supporter, I loved those occasions and all the tension which surrounded them. Remember, I didn't have a car and when we played Rangers at Celtic Park I used to get the tram from the Gorbals in the company of the fans and I knew how badly they wanted to beat Rangers. They weren't interested in turning the other cheek to anybody.

'I never considered the fans to be invading my privacy

Sent off at Brockville — still claiming innocence.

because I loved every minute of the people's involvement with the game and so did one of my greatest friends in the game, Jim Baxter. Jim was a Rangers man through and through but he was so unbiased he used to come for lunch with the Celtic players every day, which was frowned upon by his employers at Ibrox. Not that Jim bothered about that or anything else in this world! That much was demonstrated when the newspapers came out with a story that Jim was to marry one of my sisters, Bridie. The truth of the matter was that, shortly after this report appeared, Celtic were playing at home against Rangers and Bridie came along to see me play. After the game I

introduced her to the so-called 'fiancé' — and that was the first
time they had ever met!

'Anyway, after Rangers had given me a miserable start to
1963, the year grew progressively worse. Two weeks later, after
I had come back from Mass one Sunday evening, I found a
newspaperman sitting in my mother's house waiting for me. It
was the reporter who told me Celtic had received, and
accepted, a bid from Manchester United. It was the first I had
heard of any negotiations and, to be honest, I was devastated
and unwilling to go. I can say now that, if I had known Jock
Stein was going to come back to Celtic Park a couple of years
later, I would have turned down the move to Old Trafford and
stayed to become a part of the club's great days. I worshipped
the big man and had implicit faith in him but, in 1963, there
was no inkling of what was to come and there was another
incident which pushed me in the direction of Manchester
United at the time when my mind was in turmoil.

'I had cost Celtic about £25 when they got me from
Duntocher Hibs and there I was about to earn them £56,000
just over five years later, but nobody came with me from
Glasgow to Manchester when I went there for talks. Jimmy
McGrory, the manager, sent me away with Celtic's part of the
transfer agreement signed and in my pocket. That was it. My
favourite club had washed their hands of me and I hadn't fully
made up my mind that I wanted to go. Contrast that with what
greeted me on my arrival in Manchester. Not only was United's
manager, Matt Busby, there to meet me and the girl who would
later become my wife, Noreen, but he had brought along his
chairman, Louis Edwards, as well as Denis Law and his wife.
The following day, I became a Manchester United player.

'As a youngster, like a lot of Celtic supporters, I had felt a
strong bond with Manchester United and I know that persists
to this day because I can see the number of two-toned hats
scattered around Old Trafford when a match is being played,
one half coloured red for United, the other green for Celtic.
Matt Busby was a Celtic-minded man from Lanarkshire, like

Jock Stein, and his wish would have been to play for the club had that been possible. The two clubs have a similar outlook on the game and I became one of many players who have gone from Celtic Park to Old Trafford, coming after the legendary Jimmy Delaney and before such as Lou Macari and Brian McClair.'

Pat's move coincided with a time of supreme achievement for his new club, both at home and in Europe, while Celtic progressed an even more remarkable rate in Scotland and abroad.

'I was sitting at home one afternoon when a journalist from Scotland telephoned to tell me Jock Stein was to be appointed manager of Celtic and asked me for my reaction. I said then that the club would win the League Championship six times in the next seven years but even that turned out to be a conservative estimate. Big Jock had come down to Manchester only a few weeks before to see United play Everton in a U.E.F.A. Cup tie and had said to me afterwards that there was something big on the way. By the look on his face, it was fairly obvious what was happening. If Jock had asked me back to Celtic in 1965, I would have been sorely tempted, By then, though, Bobby Murdoch had developed into an outstanding player and there might have been no guarantee of a regualr game, in any case. It was Bobby Murdoch and Bertie Auld who were the architects of Celtic's recovery, too, and nobody will ever convince me otherwise.'

While Celtic's team abounded with great names and talent of the same size, Crerand was one of a gifted array at Old Trafford beside Bobby Charlton, Denis Law and the player who would, with no pun intended, have to be considered the best of the lot, George Best.

'He was the most thrilling player in the world at one stage and only one thing annoyed me about George. Why, since he had been divinely blessed with such talent, did God have to make him good-looking as well? I will tell you something about George Best, too, he was the most quietly spoken, polite man I have ever met. It was publicity and the advent of the personality cult as encouraged by television which killed his career at a tragically premature state. George was a typical Irishman in that he enjoyed a drink and the crack. One or two hours' worth of conviviality was no use to him, though, one or two days was better. George was my favourite Manchester United player and Charlie Tully was my idol at Celtic Park. Both of them were Irish, being from the different sides of Belfast, and that must say something.'

It might have been though that, having worked with Jock Stein and Matt Busby as well as players in Glasgow and Manchester who could have formed a side to beat any in the world Pat would have wanted to use the experience gained along the way in club management when his career was over. All he has to show for a career in that direction, though, is a six-month stay at Northampton Town. Like his playing days at Celtic Park, it was, coincidentally, a game played on New Year's Day which brought about the beginning of the end.

'We were due to play Preston North End, who were managed by another former Manchester United player, Nobby Stiles. It so happened I had four Scots in my team and I asked our chairman if, for that reason, the team could be put up in a hotel the night before the game. People can say this was over-reaction but I've been around long enough to know that Scots, as a race, are not to be trusted to make it through New Year's Eve in a state of tatal abstinence. The chairman, though, would have none of it and the following day we went out and lost by the only goal of the game. At time up, I was in a foul temper and told the chairman that since he would not do that small thing for me I was no longer interested in managing his club and went straight back to Manchester.

'To be frank, after Celtic Park and Old Trafford, it was hard to summon up the enthusiasm for anywhere else. As a player, the only clubs I had wanted to be with were those two and that was why I refused to accept an offer to play for Crystal Palace at the time when I retired. As a manager, I also had ambitions to be in charge of Celtic or Manchester United because they're the only two for which I feel a strong affection. When I go back to Celtic Park now I'm treated with even greater couresy than when I played there. Much as I might have been disillusioned by some of what went on when I was with the club, my attitude is once a Celtic supporter, always a Celtic supporter.

'I'll tell you how true that is, too. On the day of 25 May, 1967, a date which shouldn't require explanation, I was on a flight from Honolulu to Auckland during a marathon tour of the United States, New Zealand and Australia which Manchester United had undertaken. It was a nine-hour flight but I never once closed my eyes because my mind was not on landing in New Zealand but on what was happening in the Estadio Nacional on the outskirts of Lisbon. Davoid even of radio contact, I couldn't get out of my mind what was happening to a team made up of friends I had grown up with, like Billy, Tommy Gemmell, Bertie Auld and the rest. Our plane landed at 7.30am and I couldn't get to the hotel quick enough to put in a telephone call to the local paper, the *Auckland Star*. As you might imagine, there wasn't a soul there who had any idea what I was on about. Then, just as I was about to hang up, the switchboard operator cut in to say, 'Look, friend, I don't know who won but I did hear something about a European Cup on the early news this morning and the guy said it was the first time a British team had done it.' That was how I found out about the greatest day in Celtic's history!

'Only clubs like Celtic and Manchester United can inspire that kind of fervour. When United played Crystal Palace in the F.A. Cup final, in 1990, I was outside the tube station nearest to Wembley Stadium waiting for cousins of mine who had come over from Ireland for the game. A car stopped in front of me and all the passengers got out to ask if they could have a photograph. Each one was dressed from head to foot in red and white and topped off with a turban. Each one was a sikh! People are drawn to Celtic and Manchester United because they have a commitment to attacking football, which is something they must never lose, either. These teams should always have individuals who can lift the crowd.

'I was delighted to see Charlie Nicholas go back to Celtic for that reason. I met Charlie while on holiday in Majorca in 1983, shortly after he signed for Arsenal. My advice to him then was that, above all, he should keep a close watch on his fitness in London because there are so many distractions from the life of an athlete in that particular city. Just being back among the supporters at Celtic Park will make him a changed man, however. Charlie is the type of player needed by the game as a whole because so many matches are stifled today by rigid organisation of the type that squeezes the life out of those capable of showing invention.'

Pat Crerand was not the kind to allow that to happen to him. Regrettably, though, his time at Celtic Park coincided with a lack of direction off the field.

'We lacked the tactical advice that plays a key part in modern-day football. A wing half in my time at Celtic Park wasn't expected to cross the halfway line. I was recognised as being at my best when going forward but I wasn't given that kind of scope until I went to Manchester United. If I had known that Jock Stein was going back to the club, though . . .'

Pat Crerand   *International Appearances*

1961

May	Republic of Ireland (a)	3-0
May	Czechoslovakia (a)	0-4
October	Northern Ireland (a)	6-1
November	Wales (h)	2-0
November	Czechoslovakia (a)	2-4

1962

April	England (h)	2-0
May	Uruguay (h)	2-3
October	Wales (a)	3-2
November	Northern Ireland (h)	5-1

CHAPTER 4

Bertie Peacock

ONE MAN'S HERITAGE CAN BE ANOTHER MAN'S heresy, even when they are playing on the same side. In the Glasgow of the fifties, too, no great navigational powers would have been needed to find on which side the religious divide Celtic came down. The team had, at various stages, been received by His Holiness the Pope and the President of the Irish Free State, Eamon de Valera, as well as the perennial priest of Hollywood's imagining, Bing Crosby, while en route to the Vatican. More seriously, the club was embroiled in a bitter controversy over the flying of the flag of the Irish Republic at Celtic Park which briefly threatened their very existence over what was perceived to be a sectarian issue.

Throughout Celtic's history, however, the club, while proud of its origins and distinctive identity, has always shunned the idea of sectarianism in its employment policies. So it was that, during Celtic's Annual General Meeting in 1956 the then manager, Jimmy McGrory, could speak of three (non-Catholic) players forming what he called 'One of the greatest trios in the club's history.' One was Bobby Evans, whose energy was limitless on Celtic's behalf in whatever position he played, while another was Jock Stein. Celtic grew into being Jock's first love and he would eventually give them, and their supporters, riches that were beyond the dreams of avarice. The final member whose contribution could not be overlooked was an Ulsterman, Bertie Peacock.

In a career which spanned twelve seasons at Celtic Park, Bertie was the living embodiement of what Robert Kelly meant when the chairman addressed another A.G.M., on the sixth of September, 1957, and spoke in response to a suggestion from the less progressive side of the hall which had it that Celtic's increasingly conspicuous lack of success on the field was directly attributable to the side not containing a sufficiency of Catholic players.

A satisfactory number from the shareholders' point of view would have been no less than eleven but Kelly repeated the doctrina of the club's founding fathers which was that, as a matter of policy, Celtic would field 'the best possible team regardless of denomination.' Non-Catholics, he went on, had, throughout the club's history, played their hearts out for the team and the principle would remain the same as always.

One month later, on the 19th of October, Bertie Peacock led Celtic to their only major trophy during his captaincy, by defeating Rangers 7-1 in the League Cup final at Hampden. If ever any club policy was vindicated by the actions of its players, that game, in which half the team would have gone on any subsequent trip to Rome as tourists rather than pilgrims, was the one which did it for Celtic.

Bertie Peacock knew nothing of Glasgow and its ways when he agreed to leave his native Belfast and join Celtic in preference to either Manchester City or Arsenal, who had both shown an interest in signing him.

'They were all just names to me but I had been influenced by a man called Jack Donnelly, who was a Scot and had the distinction of being a Catholic who played for Linfield in Northern Ireland. Jack was a big Celtic man and it was because of him and Peter Connor, a friend who had played for Belfast Celtic, that I agreed terms with Jimmy McGrory. There was never any form of religious conflict at Celtic Park, though. We were all what we were and I could not have wished for a better friend than Charlie Tully, for example, and he was a Belfast Catholic from the Falls Road area. Celtic supporters were not

Bertie Peacock — 'Give a little bit, take a little bit'.

easily won over but that had nothing to do with what school you had attended. If you played well, you got the full credit that was owing to you.

Bertie was, and still is, such a mild-mannered, quietly spoken and cultivated human being that it seems distasteful having to put the sectarian question into perspective before detailing the progress of an indefatigable worker who was also capable of showing commendable versatility on Celtic's behalf on the left-hand side of the field. It was his very easygoing nature, though, which made Peacock so interesting because, on the field, he possessed a ferocious will to win that he would summarise as a willingness to 'give a little bit, take a little bit.'

Bertie was the youngest of a family of seven and when he arrived in Glasgow, in 1949, he was unsure of himself and struggled to come to terms with his new enviiroment until he was given digs in the home of the Durning family, in Carntyne Road, and was absorbed into a suitably domestic framework. In spite of being a member of the team who then defeated Rangers in the Glasgow Cup final of the 1949/50 season, Bertie did not delude himself that he had become an overnight success.

'I didn't have any craft in those days. That was something I learned at Celtic Park by never being afraid to seek, and take, advice from the more senior professionals about me and, in particular, John McPhail. John and Charlie Tully were the best of pals but while one would be giving you the benefit of his experience and undoubted ability, the other, my equally talented fellow Ulsterman, would give you the rough edge of his tongue if any mistakes were made on the park. There was one day, for instance, when Bob Kelly, who had the ultimate say in team selection and tactics, told me that, whenever I gained possession of the ball, I was to place it as near to the corner flag as possible for Charlie to run on to it and cross into the goalmouth.

'When I mentioned this to Charlie, his reply was, 'D'ye know what you can do if you drop the ball on to the corner flag? You can run and get it for yourself, that's what!'

It wasn't so much a flash of Tully wit which helped advance Bertie's career as the capricious flame of an oxy-acetylene burner, however. The apprentice plumber, who could not get out of school in Belfast quickly enough enrolled at Stow College, in Glasgow, in order to continue with his trade. One night, while carrying out a practical tst, a flash temporarily blinded Bertie in one eye, a condition which lasted for the next twenty-four hours. It was then pointed out to him that, as a first-team player, such risks and such a line of employment were no longer acceptable, and less dangerous work was found for Bertie as a physical education instructor at a school in Kilmacolm.

'It was then I started to work by day and broaden my horizons in the evening. I became very interested in the theatre, for example, and gradually made the friendships which completed my settling-in process.'

The team into which Peacock had been absorbed had developed a distressing habit of watching its challenge for the First Division Championship go out with the old year and this was the case yet again in 1951, when Celtic had gone into the first round of the Scottish Cup without a win to their credit in the month of January. The diligent, hard-working play of Peacock at inside left would be a recurring, virtuously prosaic feature of an otherwise dramatic run to Hampden and a final appearance against Motherwell, when an unusual 'cure' gave the young Irishman his first winners medal. Peacock had been blessed with strong legs and general stamina on a level so high that he had not missed a game throughout the entire season.

'I was what I would have called an everyday player with good positional sense and strength in the tackle but on the day before the final I felt weak with the symptoms of flu. Such was the way of it in those days, though, that there was no sense of panic and I was told simply to go home, rest and see how I felt in the morning. There was a Jewish businessman in Glasgow then, called Max Benjamin, who was a fervent Celtic supporter. He told me that I should take a drop of whisky, something I was no in the habit of drinking, in order to quicken the recuperative process. In the morning, the 'medicine' had taken its effect and both the manager and the chairman were quite happy for me to go out an play. They had faith in me and that counted for a lot as well. I don't think I played particularly well but I was part of a side who had a tremendous cup-fighting tradition and we knew we had to win for supporters who had suffered a lot of disappointments. We had an inspirational captain, too, in John McPhail and his goal, which was the only one of the game, was fit to win any final as he beat one man and then another before lifting the ball over Motherwell's goalkeeper, who had been forced to come off his line.'

When the St. Mungo Cup, a tournament arranged by the S.F.A. and Glasgow Corporation as part of the city's contribution towards the Festival of Britain, was added to the list of distinctions for the year, those supporters ever eager for something in which to invest their trust and optimism assumed that nothing could stand in the way of greater progress. Instead, the spectre of relegation would loom in the season that followed, though a late rally, helped significantly by the arrival of Jock Stein, from Llanelli, in Wales, removed that irritation. Better days would return sooner rather than later, too, with the help of his guidance.

'Mr McGrory was the nicest manager on the face of the earth but there were no tactics as such at Celtic Park. The attitude so far as my position was concerned was once summed up for me by the chairman. He told me if I was doing my job correctly, and my direct opponent was not having a good game, then I had fulfilled by duties in his eyes. Otherwise, the team would talk amongst themselves about any game that was to be played. Celtic Park was a place waiting to be transformed, really, and when we acquired Jock Stein we got a man who was a natural thinker on the game. He had an inner sense when it came to football because he ate and slept the game. Jock was a born leader of men and I believe I could have told you he would have gone on to achieve great things in the game as soon as I met him.'

With Stein at the helm as captain, the Coronation Cup was won in 1953, with Peacock scoring the first of the two goals which defeated Manchester United in the second of the three matches which brought the trophy to the club

'We had seen off Arsenal before then, when they had renowned players like Joe Mercer on their side and the Manchester United side of Johnny Carey and the rest was assumed to be too strong for Celtic as well. Therefore, when we beat Hibs in the final, with their forward line of Smith, Johnstone, Reilly, Turnbull and Ormond — The Famous Five

Peacock the tireless worker.

— the reaction of some of the Hibs players could not be repeated. Suffice it to say they were disgusted by what happened.'

The Coronation Cup became one of Celtic's permanent treasures and the effect of its coming was, for a time, profound.

On a personal level, it prompted the selectors of the Rest

of the World eleven to include Bertie Peacock in their team. By then, he had moved back to play at left half when it was conceded by Bertie himself that, for all his worthy attributes, he did not possess the burst of speed that was necessary for an inside forward. An understanding was then developed with Sean Fallon, which was recalled by the Republic of Ireland internationalist thus: 'Anything coming down our defensive side, I would come in behind the centre half and Bertie would drop back to cover the square ball. If Charlie (Tully) said before the game, 'I was out last night', we knew we were in trouble.'

Peacock recalls, 'You could have said many things about Charlie but he had some heart, I can tell you. Sean Fallon was a great friend and has remained so. The spirit contained within that side was such that to be at Celtic Park in those days was like being in the army. We knew we were all part of a big vlub and in our eagerness to do well for Celtic the hardest matches could be those played on the training ground. The team spirit was so strong, in fact, that when we lost a game the players would cross to the opposite side of the street if we saw a supporter that we recognised in Glasgow's town centre on our way to the restaurant where we had lunch each day.

'There was also a greater respect for each other among the players of all clubs at that time. I could have my tussles with Billy Simpson of Rangers, Don Emery from Aberdeen, or Hearts' Alfie Conn but there was not the same high incidence of serious injury. In twelve years at Celtic Park, I had only two problems and they kept me out for a total of six weeks. You never heard an opponent threaten you with a broken leg in those days. Later on, there would be some who would and I found that the most reprehensible trend imaginable. Even when we beat Rangers 7-1 in the League Cup final, the losing side went down with dignity.'

Celtic's record for a national final was a triumph of self-control, a distillation of concentration, discipline and the arts and crafts. The trophy had been won for the first time by the

Peacock chose to stay with Celtic and turn down Aston Villa.

club the season before, when Partick Thistle had been overcome, and carried on from the acquisition of the league and cup double in the 1953/54 season. The portents were good but the reality of the situation would turn out to be something altogether different.

'Key players were lost to the side. Big Jock had to retire because of injury and John McPhail had gone from the side before him. There were others who were past their peak as well. If Celtic aren't doing well now, then they buy players to get themselves out of trouble, but in the late fifties the club adhered to its policy of giving youngsters their chance. That was why what had seemed like a promising team never made the progress it might have been expected to make. Young players are fine for any side but too many of them cannot be brought in at the same time if you want to win trophies.'

In fact, Tully, Fallon and Mochan had all played their best games for Celtic and, with the problems of others, the inevitable decline started. At the start of the 1958/59 season, Billy McPhail, the bother of John, and Sean Fallon sustained the injuries which brought their careers to an end and in the ensuing turmoil both Willie Fernie and Bobby Collins asked for, and were given, transfers. Peacock's time at Celtic Park would not be long, either, yet he was still a valued member of the Northern Ireland squad who went to the World Cup finals in Sweden and had played well enough to get through to the latter stages.

'I could have moved to England immediately after those finals, in fact. My Irish team-mate, Danny Blanchflower, had gone from Aston Villa to Spurs and the Birmingham club had wanted me to take his place. However, I had a lot of respect for the chairman and what he was trying to do at Celtic Park.'

Peacock retained his will to win in spite of everything and so did the rest of the players (the season ended, ironically, with Celtic beating Hearts, thereby depriving the Edinburgh side of the Championship and giving it to Rangers by one point). What Celtic's management was trying to do was initiate a youth policy that would, in the fullness of time, produce a hand-picked, home-reared side capable of reviving the club's fortunes. There would be moments of occasional splendour but nothing of a tangible nature to justify Bob Kelly's chosen course.

Peacock, the longest-serving member of the side, had been replaced as captain by Duncan MacKay, a resourceful full-back. There was, though, a mutual respect between Bertie and his chairman and there a residual loyalty. But it was not sentimentality which kept Peacock in Celtic's side. He was commanding a place in his country's national side and it eas that status which led, indirectly to the beginning of his end at Celtic Park. The quarter-final of the Scottish Cup in 1961 had seen Hibs draw in Glasgow and force a replay at Easter Road. Peacock was not chosen for the game and his place went, instead, to the young John Clark, who had played only two games in the first team that season and the one before.

'It was hard at the time but I was hardly losing my place to a poor player, was I? John went on to prove himself with Celtic and I was left to go it on my own sooner than I had expected. In retrospect, though, I couldn't have been happier than I was at Celtic Park. At the time, I had an offer to manage Morton but I had to turn down Hal Stewart, as I did Blackpool, who knew I had a coaching badge from the F.A. coaching school at Lillieshall. If it was time to go, I decided it was best to make a clean break and return to Ireland.'

Three weeks after Celtic lost to Jock Stein's Dunfermline in the Scottish Cup final, Bertie joined Coleraine. He still lives there to this day and helps out with the training of the club.

'There are still many talented youngsters to be found in Ireland and there are also more scouts here than Baden Powell had so they shouldn't go un-noticed. It's all a question of how they mature once they move up to the senior grade.'

Bertie Peacock would be the ideal role model for any of his aspiring countrymen. He neither smoked nor drank and was careful never to put on any additional weight. A lean and hungry competitor who, like some others, helped Celtic negotiate a difficult time.

Bertie Peacock *International Appearances*

1951

October	Scotland (h)	0-3

1952

November	France (a)	1-3

1954

October	England (a)	0-2
November	Scotland (a)	2-2

1955

October	Scotland (a)	2-1
November	England (a)	0-3

1957

April	Wales (h)	0-0
April	Italy (a)	0-1
May	Portugal (h)	3-0
October	Scotland (h)	1-1
November	England (a)	3-2

1958

April	Wales (h)	0-0
June	Czechoslovakia (a)	1-0
June	Argentina (a)	1-3
June	West Germany (a)	2-2
June	France (a)	0-4
October	England (h)	3-3
November	Scotland (a)	2-2

1959

April	Wales (h)	4-1
October	Scotland (h)	4-0
November	England (a)	1-2

1960

October	England (h)	2-5
October	West Germany (h)	3-4

1961

April	Italy (a)	2-3
May	Greece (a)	1-2
May	West Germany (a)	1-2

CHAPTER 5

Tommy Gemmell

IT WAS WHILE ON HOLIDAY IN PORTUGAL, TWO decades after he had been partly instrumental in making that country permanently inextricable from Celtic's history, that Tommy Gemmell was given a reminder of one team's imperishable standing in the eyes of their supporters everywhere. Having taken shelter from a cloudburst in the company of his wife, Mary, and a welcoming drink, Tommy was then made aware of a face staring at him through the window of a pavement cafe. With his striking and much photographed features, this experience was not exactly unusual, though those who do the staring tend to forget they do not share the kind of celebrity which aids mutual recognition.

'D'ye no' remember me?' was the question asked of a man who normally had an answer for most things or at least a strong sense of diplomacy when a suitable response deserted him.

'Your face is familiar but I'm trying to put a place to it,' he said in the way that people do when they are putting a white lie before a red face.

'D'ye remember the European Cup final in Lisbon?' continued his acquaintance, asking a question that was as rhetorical as it is possible to get. 'The Celtic team bus got stuck in a traffic jam on the way to the ground? Our supporters' bus drew up beside yours and I waved to you through the window. D'ye remember me noo?'

Personal identification with a time, place or era is the prerogative of a large support, but this was surely taking association with a team, or individual, to an illogical degree. However, not for the first time, and certainly not for the last, Tommy Gemmell had been given cause to reflect that what happened on 25 May, 1967, when Celtic defeated Inter Milan, was effectively the most important and influential day in Celtic's existence . . . .

The legend of the side who forego individual personalities to assume the collective identity of the Lisbon Lions can, according to Gemmell, be viewed in two, polarised, ways, depending upon who is doing the looking and for what reason. The achievement can be regarded as an albatross round the neck of the club when it is held up as defining a standard beneath which Celtic should not fall, or to which they should always aspire, no matter what. On the other hand, it can be used as a source of inspiration for every Celtic player who has come after the European cup-winning side. Gemmell subscribes to the latter school of thought because, in his estimation, what happened inside the Estadio Nacional was a triumph for the working class of the industrial West of Scotland as represented by Celtic. It was also a testimony to the sense of organisation and team spirit which had been non-existent when he first arrived at Celtic Park six years earlier.

The young Tommy Gemmell had begun to work as an apprentice electrician at the Ravenscraig steelworks near to his home in Motherwell when Celtic showed an interest in signing him. He has never forgotten, far less tried to deny, those origins, or lost his feelings of gratitude to football for enabling him to broaden his horizons, and improve his standard of living, while being among that community.

'The first time I had the opportunity to travel outside of Scotland was because of football. I had been chosen as part of a junior select to play a representative match in Dublin. That was in 1960 and those were far less sophisticated times for players who were not as worldly as today's generation. When

Gemmell — The apprentice electrician who became a bright spark at Celtic Park.

our team assembled for our first meal together at the hotel in Ireland, I kept my mouth shut and pretended to be looking about me when the waiter came to take our orders in case I suffered a fall from the social graces.

'There was another player, though, who was not so self-conscious. He perused the menu and then announced, to a fairly predictable response from the rest of us, that he would have a various omelette. Luckily, he knew his way about the pitch far better than he did a menu and went on to become a world-famous name.'

It was during another representative match staged at Motherwell's Fir Park that Gemmell was able to gain access to the game at a higher level.

'I had one of those nights when absolutely nothing went wrong and after the match the scouts of three different clubs wanted to meet me. When I say that one of them was from Brentford and another was from Port Vale, that is not to make fun of them. In fact, their interest was indicative of the talent that was available then to all clubs throughout the country and illustrated how hard it was to step up to the senior game. I never thought of myself as an exceptionally gifted player. I was fit and my tackling was good, with strong shooting ability being another point in my favour. I never forget, though, that I was lucky, too. Some players who were a lot better than I was never got the chance. In any case, Celtic's scout was wise enough to let Port Vale and Brentford have their say and then come in to tell me that, with my ability, there was only one club fit enough to have me. The scout's name was Eddie McArdle and he was well known to everybody in our area because he was a local councillor who went on to become Provost of Motherwell and Wishaw, though not just because he signed me for Celtic! Being a politician, Eddie was shrewd enough to know that the final man in also makes the most lasting impression. By using the same personal technique and keeping my mother and father happy, Eddie had signed the likes of Billy McNeill and Bobby Murdoch from that part of Lanarkshire and he convinced everyone that it was the right thing to let me go to Celtic Park.'

The Gemmell family had been steeped in the local side, Motherwell, and Tommy can recall being able to recite, parrot fashion, the names of the team members who had brought the Scottish Cup to Fir Park at Dundee's expense in 1952. His own place on the terracing that day had been denied Tommy by his father, who reasoned that the big crowd at Hampden would frighten such a youngster. The idea of Tommy Gemmell being put off by the size of a crowd anywhere would eventually turn out to be a fanciful notion but it would also be some time before the theory would be put to the test, given the nature of his progress and the state of the club he found at Celtic Park when he went there in 1961.

'Celtic trained athletes, but not footballers, in those days. There was endless lapping of the track but no work with the ball or any special attention paid to tactics. It would have to be said that it showed. What made matters worse, of course, was that Rangers were then enjoying all the success that was going. This was not to say they had all the best players, too, because the vast majority of the side who would become the Lisbon Lions were all with Celtic at that time. We lacked proper leadership, though. I can remember the side going to Ireland once to play in a friendly on Glentoran's ground and watching Charlie Gallagher being told to come out for the second half of a friendly game. As Robert Kelly, who was then Celtic's chairman, took his seat in the stand and scanned the pitch to find Charlie doing his warming-up exercises, the word was suddenly delivered from the directors' box that Gallagher was not to get a game at all and he had to troop off disconsolately. Having said that, it would be impossible to criticise Sir Robert, as he later became, for his work on Celtic's behalf, or Jimmy McGrory, who was then manager of the team, because they always acted out of what they thought were Celtic's best interests.'

Results at home and abroad suggested Celtic was a club with a will of its own, since it was frequently carried in directions so unpredictable it was obvious there was more than one hand on the tiller. When Gemmell signed, it had been four years since Celtic last won a trophy and it would be another three years before they knew the feeling again. It was a time for assertiveness, though, rather than run the risk of being part of the high turnover in staff which can accompany times of turmoil like that. If Tommy Gemmell will forever be remembered for flamboyancy and the more positive aspects of the game, he can recall paying attention to the more pressing business of making an impact. His first Old Firm confrontation came in a reserve game at Ibrox in which his direct opponent was a Scottish internationalist uncertain of his own future with Rangers and also hindered by having a 'heart the size of an aspirin'. Gemmell made his mark with the relish of someone striving to be noticed.

'My father insisted I finish my apprenticeship at Ravenscraig, therefore I was a part-timer with Celtic while trying to make the first team. Two nights a week I would come out of the steelworks and get on a bus from Motherwell to Glasgow, being fast asleep before the final destination of Glasgow Cross. In the earliest days, when I was being paid £2 a week as a provisional signing, I couldn't afford the cost of the tram ride which ought to have completed the journey from there to Celtic Park. It was then a case of running the last lap before walking back after training and falling fast asleep again on the way home. The extra £2 I was making was enough to give me a good night out at the Trocadero dance hall in Hamilton, though, and I could appreciate then that I would rather work at Celtic Park than Ravenscraig.'

That choice might have been a debatable one for those who watched a side capable of winning 5-1 at Pittodrie on Tommy's first-team debut but saw them lose 4-0 to M.T.K. Budapest in the old-style Fairs Cup after taking a three-goal lead to Hungary.

Eight months after that embarrassing episode, it was confirmed, however, that Jock Stein would be returning to Celtic Park from Hibs as manager. It was all the encouragement Tommy needed to fully develop his personality, since Stein was known to like full backs who overlapped.

'In big Jock's first game, which was against Airdrie at Broomfield, I was up and down that park like a conventional winger and, by half-time, we were two goals in front. I went into the dressing room feeling very pleased with myself but the

Stein's first words took the smile off Gemmell's face.

big man's first words soon took the smile off my face, because it was pointed out to me that my first job was to defend properly. In order to make sure the lesson had sunk in sufficiently, the manager gave me one more game, which we lost, and then dropped me altogether. He knew that would have the effect of settling me down because the Scottish Cup final against Dunfermline was just over a month away and getting to Hampden was all that mattered to me.'

Gemmell, though, did not possess the kind of personality that could be subdued for long. Central to his character was an unshakable confidence which led him to believe that there was no such thing as an opponent who started any game with the ability to get the better of him for the majority of the ninety minutes. Or, as his contemporary, Bobby Lennox, put it: 'Big Tam thought he was the best man in the team and he wasn't slow to let you know about it.'

'There were very few I thought able to cause me any problems,' says Gemmell. 'In my earliest days, Sandor, the winger from M.T.K. Budapest, tore me inside out in the European semi-final lost by Celtic. There were two others, Kenny Aird at St. Johnstone and Partick Thistle's Ian Cowan, who threatened to give me a hard time but were never able to sustain the effort.

'The one who gave me most trouble was a veteran, Johnny Hamilton of Hearts, who was as good with his mouth as he was with his feet. When Celtic met them at Tynecastle, Jim Kennedy was playing in front of me and before the game started he shouted within earshot of Johnny words to the effect that he was not to get past me under any circumstances.

' ''Dinnae you listen to him, son. Just you concentrate on playing your own game,'' was Johnny's reply. A real con-man.

'The Celtic side who won the Scottish Cup in 1965 and then set out the following season on winning the first League Championship of nine in a row all felt supremely confident, though. We never had any team talks after Jock Stein got us into a style of play that had us telepathic in our understanding of each other, and it was also possible for us to predict the winning margin before we started paying certain games. The only time humility came into it was during the season when we won every competition we entered. I used to pick up John Clark and Jimmy Johnstone in my car on the way in from Lanarkshire, and over the months our conversations moved from the wistful to the mildly hysterical. We started off by saying, "we could win everything here" but without any real sense of conviction. By the time the League Cup and the Glasgow Cup had been won, someone would inevitably start off the morning conversation by saying "wouldn't it be great to get to the European Cup final?" After Dukla Prague had been taken care of in the semi-final, the mood changed to "wouldn't it be wonderful to beat Inter Milan?" '

Tommy says he can recall with absolute clarity the events of 25 May, 1967 and without recourse to tele-prompting. The lead-up to the match is also as vivid as anything that took place on the park. The clamour around the Estadio Nacional was precisely to his liking, first of all, complete with traffic jam and waves from supporters' buses which were, apparently, the start of lifelong friendships.

'I had one pre-match ritual and that was to stand outside Celtic Park or any other ground where we were playing until the last possible moment, chatting to friends and getting the buzz of the crowd as they started to arrive. In that respect, I was totally different from someone like Stevie Chalmers, the scorer of our other goal in Lisbon. Stevie would be inside the dressing room an hour before the kick-off and completely kitted out and ready for the start five minutes after that. In Lisbon, we arrived with forty-five minutes to go until the game began, and when the two teams approached the stairs that led up to the pitch the adrenalin was pumping furiously. When Bertie Auld decided to start singing the Celtic Song in front of the Italians they were mystified and we were ready to take them apart. In my opinion, that is precisely what we did, too. Their goalkeeper, Sarti, should have been awarded the V.C. for the way he kept the score down. It could, and should, have been 6-1 for Celtic because we were that much better than they were.'

'It was Jock Stein, with his sense of occasion and often stunning perceptiveness, who made two memorable statements prior to the start of the night of revelry which followed Celtic's triumph. In the first instance Stein said the Lisbon Lions would never be beaten by any other team. This was not an untypical boast but a protective assurance that those players would never be put on the same field again so that their memory would remain untarnished for posterity. He was as good as his word. It was also the manager's assertion that the game would never be the same again for the eleven involved. The magnitude of their achievement was such that Stein could sense it would leave an indelible mark on their subconscious. Tommy Gemmell had, on the one hand, carefully cultivated what the players of Inter Milan would ruefully have called braggadocio, the swaggering image of West of Scotland gallousness, from the time of his introduction to the first team. It had been nurtured by attending every supporters' club function he could and perfecting what amounted to a theatrical routine in front of an always highly appreciative audience in the 'Jungle' at Celtic Park.

'I would go through my repertoire of winks and exaggerated gestures for the benefit of the crowd and usually at the expense of the linesman in front of them, but at the same time I would be speaking to him in stage whispers and explaining that it was all an act. The crowd loved me and I knew it. When physical comparisons started to be made between me and Danny Kaye, I decided to keep my hairstyle the way it was and gladly accept attention being drawn to the size of my nose.'

The less appealing side of being in the public eye, however, is the trouble that comes from those who have no reason to share in the demonstration of affection. Gemmell would freely admit to having had a fairly memorable two weeks of celebration following the winning of the European Cup, for instance, but compared with the carousing indulged in by those who watched the game this was almost monastic self-denial. The image Tommy had, though, was of a high liver who hunted, shot and fished when he wasn't leading an active social life or going through seven cars in four years.

Gemmell makes Airdrie pay the penalty.

'I was much younger then, of course, but a lot of the stories got out of proportion. At one time, I disliked lager so much I used to take it with lime to kill the taste. If that proved to be a passing phase, my drinking habits were far removed from the tales of me allegedly shifting a bottle of vodka per day. Very few of the Lisbon Lions could honestly have been described as saints in that respect. It was always a case of live hard, play hard with us. The team, though, was also full of enthusiastic trainers who were also fortunate to have a manager who could make going to your work an enjoyable experience.'

Tommy Gemmell's regard for Jock Stein was, professionally speaking, unbounded. The player's removal from Celtic Park would come about, however, because of an incident abroad which led to the gradual erosion of that relationship. Stein, after his salutary chastisement of the player at Airdrie, had always known the value of Gemmell's self-belief and the influential ripples it would cause to spread throughout the rest of the team and on to the terracing. Because he was loathed by a Rangers support who found it difficult to come to terms with a Protestant being so committed to their downfall, Tommy was, in the conventional way of these matters, adored by Celtic supporters brought up on such gregariousness from their favourites.

'The Rangers fans started to dislike me because they thought I kicked Willie Henderson upside-down in our games. I can say with all honesty I never deliberately hurt wee Willie and he would verify that statement. We were genuinely as friendly as our publicity made us out to be. Perhaps it couldn't happen today but after an Old Firm game we would meet in a pub called Reids in Hope Street and have a few pints before going our separate ways. The most frequently heard chant in those days, though, was "Gemmell's a bastard". When my mother heard the Rangers fans chant those words for the first time, she became so upset she vowed never to go back to an Old Firm game, and she was as good as her word. It was as well for her sake that I had moved into a house of my own by then because I also had a milk-boy who wore a Rangers scarf and gave that particular chant a rasping rendition every morning at the crack of dawn.'

His immense popularity was unaffected by the scandalous World Club Championship final in which Celtic succumbed to the provocation thrust at them over three games against the South American side, Racing Club of Argentina.

Gemmell was not one of the four Celtic players sent off out of a total of six in the infamous play-off match, held in Montevideo, but in the midst of the turmoil that punctuated the game he had dispensed summary justice of his own against an opponent, Raffo, who had otherwise evaded censure. The incident was captured by the television cameras and thereafter shown at regular intervals as Sir Robert Kelly, a strict disciplinarian, fined every player £250. It would take a similar incident to bring about the beginning of the end for Gemmell at Celtic Park. While playing for Scotland in a World Cup qualifying tie against West Germany, Tommy clashed with Helmut Haller in an identically public way. To this day, he would maintain that his actions were those of a man brought to the end of his tether by the taunting of an opponent, something Tommy felt should have been apparent to the watching Jock Stein.

Adored by Celtic
fans, others had
another word for
Gemmell.

'The Saturday after that match was the League Cup final
between ourselves and St. Johnstone. I had overcome the
disappointment of losing the international and what happened
with Haller and was looking forward to a game in what was
then regarded as Celtic's lucky tournament. As usual, I was
standing outside Hampden savouring the atmosphere but when
I got back to the dressing room to change, the first person I met
was Jim Kennedy, who handed me two complimentary tickets

for the stand. At the same time I could see the young David Hay putting on the shorts with my number on them. The message was obvious: I had been disciplined by the club in the form of being dropped from the Cup Final. It was not a decision I could accept, or respect. It was an unwritten law at Celtic Park that if someone was sent off he automatically missed out on our next game. However, although I was sent off in the international I found the manager's way of teaching me a lesson a less than acceptable one.

'Jock had said nothing from the end of the international until the game at Hampden, even though we had been on the same aeroplane back to Scotland and had then been in each other's company for three days at Seamill, Celtic's traditional pre-Cup final headquarters. I telephoned the manager first thing on the Sunday morning and asked him one simple question: 'Would you have left me out if we had been playing Rangers and not St. Johnstone?' I got the impression there was hesitation in his voice before Jock denied that the opposition made any difference. When I pressed him for an explanation, he told me to come into Celtic Park and the upshot was that I asked Celtic for a transfer. Even though the request was later withdrawn, my friendship with Jock had been irreparably damaged.'

Stein had it in mind to dismantle the Lisbon Lions and those who were on the fringes of that side from the moment Ove Kindvall scored the goal in extra time that defeated Celtic in the European Cup final of 1970. In spite of going a goal in front, scored by Gemmell, Celtic's performance was made to look naive and their preparation was, for once, able to be called into doubt as such as Kindvall and Van Hanegem threatened to run riot against players who looked at them as if they were ghosts. Because stories began to circulate the following day that the team had been more concerned with money than anything else, Celtic's failure was blamed on greed having had an adverse effect. Tommy would refute those suggestions by saying that very little money was made out of

Lisbon and that it was the same story in Milan against Feyenoord. Stein had resolved to create another team and make way for the burgeoning young talent surrounding him at Celtic Park. Within a short space of time, Willie Wallace, Stevie Chalmers, John Hughes and John Clark had gone, soon to be followed by Gemmell.

'I never wanted to leave Celtic but players like Jim Brogan and Jimmy Quinn were starting to get a game in front of me and it was perfectly clear I was no longer needed. What had been achieved at Celtic Park in a relatively short space of time was such, though, that there are supporters who still need to be reminded that I went on to play for Nottingham Forest. In a way, a part of me died when I left Celtic, too. The City Ground, in Nottingham, was like a Butlins holiday camp compared to what I had been used to under Jock Stein and, after fulfilling the two years of my contract there, I came back to Scotland and Dundee.

It is a testimony to the high regard in which Tommy was held by Celtic's support that they never lost their respect for him even though he inflicted serious damage on his former team as both player and manager at Dens Park. The League Cup final of 1973 was won by a Dundee side captained by Gemmell, who felt embarrassed by having to receive the trophy in front of those more used to seeing him in a hooped jersey. The League championship was lost seven years later when the Dundee team managed by Tommy scored a remarkable 5-1 win at Dens Park. Four days later he was sacked. For all that his image could often be a frivolous one, Tommy had an affinity with the game itself which went deeper than luxuriating in its more glamorous rewards. Having moved into a new career in insurance, he could not resist the call to help out the lowly Albion Rovers, whose reputation was as threadbare as their strips and their future as bleak as their ground in Coatbridge. As well as bringing the lessons of Stein to Cliftonhill, Gemmell introduced a measure of financial stability to a club where that was an alien concept. A total of £73,000 was taken in from transfer fees from the sale of players to Clydebank's Jack Steedman and Willie Harkness at Queen of the South. Those two club figureheads have always been renowned for attending to fiscal matters with religious zeal.

In one case, Gemmell kept Queen of the South's team bus waiting outside Cliftonhill until the approach of midnight while he reeled in a transaction that was more generous to Albion Rovers. Such victories over the system's best players might be thought as meritorious, certainly as hard fought, as the goings on inside the Estadio Nacional. A life in club management is not secure, though, and, with an insurance man's awareness of the future, Tommy was by then intent on letting his life take on a different rhythm. For him, perfection now would be early retirement followed by three days' fishing per week and the rest of the time to himself.

'I would still be able to turn up at Celtic Park in that way because I have never lost the thrill I get every time I walk through that door. I will always be Tommy Gemmell of Celtic in the eyes of most people and that's fine by me because that is how I think of myself. If I had to sum up my life in the game, in fact, it would be by saying that I loved every minute of it and I wish I hadn't given up playing as soon as I did.'

Tommy Gemmell *International Appearances*

1966

April	England (h)	3-4
October	Wales (a)	1-1
November	Northern Ireland (h)	2-1

1967

April	England (a)	3-2
May	U.S.S.R. (h)	0-2
October	Northern Ireland (a)	0-1

1968

February	England (h)	1-1
October	Denmark (a)	1-0
November	Austria (h)	2-1

1969

April	West Germany (h)	1-1
May	Wales (a)	5-3
May	Northern Ireland (h)	1-1
May	England (a)	1-4
May	Cyprus (h)	8-0
September	Eire (a)	1-1
October	West Germany (a)	2-3

1970

April	England (a)	0-0

1971

February	Belgium (a)	0-3

CHAPTER 6

Bertie Auld

'WORK IS WHAT YOU DO FROM MONDAY TO Friday. On Saturday, you get the day off to play fitba' — Bertie Auld, during his heyday at Celtic Park, describing the life of a professional footballer.

Maryhill's most widely acknowledged feature of an eccentric note is thought to be the fact that it is the geographical location of Partick Thistle. Bertie Auld is living proof that this is only half right.

If the area to the North West of Glasgow ever had such a thing as a cultural attaché, then the player with the loping gait and the jutting jaw with the permanent seven o'clock shadow was the holder of that post. It was Celtic's good fortune, twice over, that the unique talent he possessed was never put to use in a red and yellow jersey, though, but in his beloved green and white hoops. Celtic made, and eventually broke, Bertie in the 'fifties and then brought him back as a more mature individual to be one of the main orchestrators behind the side that took the club out of a long, barren period that would have been beyond the understanding of those who were reared on the undiluted achievement of the modern era which he helped start. If Celtic has an aura which, once it has touched the individual, breeds in him a slavish devotion to the club, regardless of background, Bertie Auld epitomised the effects of that spell on the unsuspecting.

Auld — 'On Saturdays you get the day off to play fitba'.

Panmure Street, which overlooked Partick Thistle's ground, was no different from any other of its time. For the male population resident there, football was the primary source of recreation from morning until night in the days when it was still possible to be chased by the police for playing within the precincts of Glasgow's tenements and fined by the courts if turn of speed was not sufficient to evade capture. The 'Harry Wraggs,' as Partick Thistle were known to their supporters when the team did not leave them bereft of words, had first claim on Bertie's affections.

He was the third of seven children belonging to Joe and Margaret Auld. The former was a bricklayer's labourer and unrivalled mentor to the most precociously gifted of his offspring, while the latter was known with deep affection only as 'Ma' to her son from the first time he gained acclaim as a player until she took a matriarchal interest in her boy's colourful career in management at Firhill. The street where Bertie lived also overflowed with an abundance of such naturally gifted players that it eventually spawned its own side, who played in the local amateur league under a name which betrayed the aspirations of its members, Panmure Thistle. By the age of sixteen, though, Bertie's prowess would belong to one of the two junior clubs in the area, Maryhill Harp. After only six games at that level, however, Bertie's progress was so remarkable that he was invited to Celtic Park for signing talks.

'I had played as an amateur for the Harp and in those days that meant anybody going up to the senior grade was entitled to pocket all of the transfer fees from the club in question. Where I came from, it was possible that anyone suddenly finding himself with two bob might not be seen again for a few days. The statutory signing-on fee of £200 therefore represented a fortune. It was on the way to Celtic Park, though, that my father, who was a highly principled man unlikely to compromise himself no matter how much we could have done with the money, told me I was to sign for the Harp first of all on a form that would guarantee them the transfer fee and give me the obligatory signing-on fee of just £25. He said that was only fair since the Harp had given me the platform to show a club like Celtic how I could play. Once that arrangement had been reached with Jimmy McGrory, who was then Celtic's manager, he asked my father what he wanted to drink and the deal to settle my future was celebrated over a 'hauf' of whisky.'

The contract could not be signed, though, because the young Auld was still three weeks short of the statutory seventeen years of age. The legal loophole able to be exploited there, however, was covered over by one more act of parental guidance. The day after the head of the family had given Celtic his word, a scout representing Partick Thistle arrived in Panmure Street and said that Davie Meiklejohn, the club's manager, wanted a word with Bertie. Instead, Meiklejohn got a visit from his legal guardian while the sought-after youngster sat outside the manager's office. The blandishments of Partick Thistle's cocktail cabinet were not enough to weaken resolve, however, and the fact that Bertie Auld would be lost to Firhill as a player eventually had to be accepted with customary good grace.

'My father knew his football and Partick Thistle in particular. At that time, the likes of Tommy Ewing and Davie McParland, who were not much older than me, were starting to make an impact at Firhill in what was my position. I was instructed that I would get a better chance of a career in the game if I went to be an apprentice to the big names who were at Celtic Park, like Charlie Tully, Bertie Peacock, Willie Fernie and Jock Stein himself. The first time I saw Celtic Park was the day I met Mr McGrory with my father but, within a month, I looked upon the place as my home and was made to realise at the same time what the club meant to the people who supported them. Neighbours I had only a nodding acquaintance with in Panmure Street would walk me up the road every day when I came back from training so that they could, in some small way, feel a bigger part of what went on behind those big, green doors at the front of the old stand. I was a home bird by nature and that feeling of belonging was so important to me it left an indelible mark where Celtic was concerned.'

The year was 1955 and Celtic's domestic record was one of sporadic distinction. The decade would close with only one more, albeit imperishable memory, when the League Cup was won against Rangers by the exotic margin of 7-1, and then the years would see Celtic slip into a deep sleep of the kind which made their plight a matter of private grief for those who supported them.

'No matter what was, or was not, going on at Celtic Park,

though, I was made to understand that Celtic played in a certain way and the players conducted themselves in a manner befitting ambassadors for the club, even if they were only walking down Sauchiehall Street. It was the era of the Teddy Boy and the fashion was for drape jackets and drainpipe trousers. I can remember one of my sisters buying me a suit from the Caledonian Tailors, which meant that it didn't come cheaply. Going on to the team bus for a reserve match one day, I was taken aside by our trainer, Jimmy Gribben, and told that if I didn't turn up in more suitable clothing the following week I would no longer play for Celtic.'

It was not so much Bertie's dress sense as his wayward nature on the field which separated him from the club for the first time. Before his name had appeared in the first team, Dumbarton asked Jimmy McGrory if the teenager could be taken until the end of the season. There was no such thing then as a loan agreement and formal transfer forms had to be signed. Bertie had watched several other young players leave Celtic Park in that manner and had never counted one of them back in again. In career terms, it seemed the grisly equivalent of the patient's bed being moved nearest to the door of the hospital ward.

'Once again, though, my father had the foresight to tell me that this was a marvellous opportunity to make even quicker progress and he was absolutely correct. I played against Celtic on one occasion and did well up against Mike Hughney, who was then an established first-team player. Dumbarton also had a lengthy cup run that season and it was when that came to an end Jimmy McGrory invited me to sign for Celtic a second time and I made my debut against Rangers at Ibrox in a Glasgow Cup tie. Even in the reserve side I was made to realise what playing for Celtic was all about in the days when those games were watched by crowds in excess of 30,000 people. Playing beside someone like John McPhail was an education, for instance. His favourite saying to me was, 'Hey, sir, are you playin' for claps?' if he felt I was pandering to the crowd instead of doing what was best for the team.'

Bertie — A willingness to entertain at all times.

If Bertie showed a willingness to entertain at all times, he also had an unfailing capacity for allowing himself to be goaded into misbehaviour and displaying an undisciplined streak which put his name in the mental file carried about in the head of Celtic's chairman, Robert Kelly, who put the club's good reputation before all other considerations.

'However, I took the attitude that each game for Celtic was a test of loyalty in what was a hard school. Playing against someone like Bobby Shearer, of Rangers, you would have needed shinguards on the back of your head but I would admit that I was a naughty boy. The love I had for Celtic, though, would never allow me to give anything less than one hundred per cent, and that applied to second-team games as well.'

The proof of both those statements could be found in the

circumstances of Bertie's eventual departure for Birmingham City, for a fee of £15,000, in 1961. An opportunity to join Bobby Collins in a double transfer to Everton had been turned down at the last moment because of a reluctance to bow to the inevitable and admit that his chairman saw no future for him at Celtic Park. As well as that, Bertie had hoped that his engagement to his future wife, Liz, would hint at a significant change of personality to the hierarchy at the club. It did not. On the night that Celtic lost to Dunfermline in a Scottish Cup final replay, the ostracised Bertie was busily scoring a hat-trick for the reserves against Hearts at Tynecastle. After the game, Birmingham's manager, Gil Merrick, formalised the details of the unwanted forward's transfer and the next day the pair found themselves in New Street station. The move would have a pivotal effect on his life but had the most inauspicious of beginnings which threatened, momentarily, to bring his career to an end.

'I went up to my room in the Midland Hotel and put my suitcase down on the bed, leaving it unopened. I went downstairs and had my dinner before returning to my room, lifting my suitcase and walking straight out of the hotel once again. My intention was quite simple: I was going home because I didn't think I could cope with life outside of Glasgow. It was the likes of Paddy Crerand and John Colrain at Celtic Park who had to show me around my own city centre because they were from places like the Gorbals and the Calton and I was from the more remote district of Maryhill. The thought of having to exist without close family, friends and fiancée was too much to handle and I walked along Corporation Street in Birmingham to get the train back home again. It was then I caught sight of my own reflection, holding on to my suitcase, in the window of a car showroom. It brought me back to my senses because it was like looking into a mirror. The choice was a simple one; If I went back, I was putting myself out of football. The alternative was, quite simply, to grow up. I went back to the hotel and when I got up

Bertie — Playing out of his skin.

in the morning and found Gil Merrick waiting for me in the foyer to keep me company over breakfast I realised that good people were good people, no matter where they came from, and settled down to four informative years at Birmingham City.'

The problems with his temperament which had disrupted Bertie's prospects with Celtic made the journey with him, though, and a series of orderings off followed, both in domestic and European football. The most damaging incident was that involving the England internationalist, Johnny Haynes, during a game with Fulham. After having been dismissed, Bertie, who ought to have known better, clashed with Haynes, who would have known better after that, as he left the field. A ban of 28 days was imposed by the Football League and the opinion held by Robert Kelly, that the player was an intractable type unlikely to mellow with age, seemed to have been vindicated. So far as playing the game was concerned, however, Bertie was attaining the maturity that had been given to him partly by virtue of playing in a less frantic atmosphere.

'Trading kick for kick was not something that was brought into being in Scotland along with the introduction of the Premier League. There was always a difference between the tempo of the game in England and what we accepted as being normal and I began to revel in the greater time I had on the ball, learning to get the dust of the touchline off my boots and how to make passes from further inside the park, which converted me into an inside left as opposed to a winger.'

Marriage and the birth of a daughter, Susan, did the rest so far as bringing about the change in Bertie's personality that would ultimately convert the man who thought he was a lost cause.

'The Scottish League had played their English equivalent at Villa Park, in Birmingham, and I had gone along to congratulate the players and officials on their 4-3 win. In the team's hotel, I found Jock Stein sitting with Robert Kelly and a brief conversation, which was far more meaningful than I could ever have imagined, took place. Jock was still manager of Hibs at that stage but within weeks it was announced that he would be leaving Easter Road to take over at Celtic Park. It was then I received a telephone call at home from someone called Dougie Hepburn, who was a good friend of the big man's. Robert Kelly had found me a changed man and Jock had said he would like to bring me back. Dougie came right out and asked me how I felt about returning to Celtic. Birmingham had an F.A. Cup tie to play against West Ham the following day but my answer was, 'Do you want me in Glasgow tonight?'

When the time did come to make that journey, Auld, as he had done ten years earlier, signed yet another contract for Jimmy McGrory in what was his last official act as manager of Celtic. The tangible proof of his anxiety over returning to that particular club once again lay in the conditions of his agreement, which paid the player a basic wage that was £5 a week less than he had been getting at Birmingham.

'My attitude to Celtic, and football in general, was that it was primarily about having fun and giving entertainment to people who had paid to watch the play. It was important to attain a reasonable standard of living but that was not the main reason for being in the game, unlike today. There are players now, even at Celtic Park, who go into contractual negotiations looking for a signing-on fee, special bonuses and perhaps the promise of a testimonial at some later date. Whatever happened to the loyalty test and playing for the hoops?

'Jock Stein knew that, whatever I got up to, he couldn't hurt me by taking away my wages or doing anything of that kind. What affected me most of all was not getting the chance to play for Celtic. When I came back from Birmingham there was an incident in which I sat on the ball at Shawfield during a game with Clyde because none of their players would come to challenge me. I looked over at the dug-out, expecting to see a favourable acknowledgement from Jock but those big miner's hands had been clenched into fists and his humour wasn't helped when he bumped his head off the roof of the dug-out while trying to get out and really let me know what he thought! I believed the crowd would love my antics, and they did, but Jock was incensed and told me in the dressing room afterwards that I had humiliated my fellow professionals and he found that totally unacceptable. The big man wouldn't let me play the following Saturday and sent me to look at Partick Thistle instead on the basis that we had a game coming up against them. He knew, though, that I would be distracted from watching the game by spending the entire afternoon explaining to all and sundry why I wasn't playing for Celtic.'

The relationship between Stein and Auld, and that between the player and Celtic's chairman was, one fall from grace in the United States apart, at the stage of comfortable understanding. Stein had, in the 'fifties, played in the same Celtic team as Auld on a couple of occasions which have faded into the recesses of Bertie's mind. The pair would, in the course of their second collaboration, achieve the unforgettable together. Auld was also the recipient of more tolerant understanding from Robert Kelly, who, from the time of their meeting in the Birmingham hotel, had detected that this was a changed man with whom he could do business.

'The chairman would come up to me and make small talk. It was nothing earth-shattering but an indication that things had changed and I had been fully accepted as a member of the family. On the park, players like Stevie Chalmers and Jimmy Johnstone were beginning to break through but they needed an experienced man with Celtic at heart to help them come together. Jock Stein had changed, too. The ideas he had put across the table at Ferrari's restaurant, in Glasgow, where the Celtic players had their pre-match meal, had started to get delivered more forcefully on the training ground. It was Jock's idea to use Bobby Murdoch and myself in a midfield partnership that made sure we were not too divorced from the action at any stage. McKellar/Watt I liked to call our association, because we were Celtic's link men. At our best, as in the European Cup final against Inter Milan in 1967, we could have played blindfold and still found each other with the ball.'

Auld's non-visible influence on the team was his attitude. He was incorrigibly confident and had the maturity to carry it off. It was Auld who started the singing of the Celtic Song in the subterranean tunnel of the Estadio Nacional in Lisbon, much to the astonishment of the Inter Milan players. The climax of that game, which even Jock Stein's nerves could not take, forcing the manager to record the one and only time he turned his back on a football match and walked away to the dressing room before the end, involved Auld taking the ball for a walk to use up valuable seconds and keep the opposition hemmed in at a corner flag in their own half of the field. Bertie's mind was full of such demoralising mischief. Years earlier, during a game Birmingham had needed to win to avoid relegation, Bertie had trotted over to take a corner kick in the dying seconds. To the amazement of everyone in the ground, he booted the ball further down the touchline and out for a throw-in to the other side. By the time they had worked out what was going on, the referee had blown for time up.

Confidence was matched by an equally deceptive quickness. Bertie could look like the archetypal Glaswegian whose only problem appeared to be that his shorts had not been fitted with pockets into which he could thrust his hands as he sauntered all over the pitch but goals would come regularly through sudden acceleration. Two of the three which brought Celtic the Scottish Cup in 1965 and afforded them an exit from the long, dark tunnel of the previous eight years were as a result of that asset. If it is considered, too, that the Premier Division record for the most number of goals scored by the champions is 90, shared by Dundee United in 1983 and Celtic in 1988, Stein's side of the 'sixties was phenomenally prolific. In the first three full seasons of Stein's management, Celtic won the title each time and scored a total of 323 goals and in the process, 106 in the 1965/66 season, 111 goals a year later and 106 goals in the championship after that.

'Big Jock never mentioned records but whenever the team got close to a new distinction the subject would suddenly be introduced. It doesn't surprise me, either, that the goalscoring rate is dwindling in the Premier Division, even though teams there have two more games to play than we did in the set-up which existed before league reconstruction. If teams have to play each other four times a season and it becomes obvious that one is far superior to another, then the instinct for self-preservation will become even more apparent. If someone keeps hitting you and giving you a bloody nose, then the only thing you can do is defend yourself.'

The reputation Bertie had as an entertainer was, in later years, blemished by the criticism which came his way for the ultra-defensive nature of the clubs he managed. It is a charge he vigorously denies but it is ironic that the incident which should have begun his career in coaching should have occurred at Easter Road when he was instructing Hibs' reserve players on how to avoid losing a goal.

Six years to the day after he had rejoined Celtic, Bertie was allowed to go to the Edinburgh club as his appearances under Stein became increasingly less frequent and usually confined to European competition, where his cerebral approach was still valuable. Auld also found Eddie Turnbull, Hibs' manager, a tactician he could respect as much as Stein and the regard became mutual the morning that the manager overheard Auld explaining to a group of youngsters the rudiments of keeping their goal out of harm's way. A job was found on the coaching staff for Auld even though Bertie would refer, jocularly, to Turnbull as 'The Growler' since he had such an abrasive manner that he 'wouldn't have given you a look at a bird's nest in case you told somebody.'

Tony Higgins, now the full-tme secretary of the Scottish Professional Footballers Association, was one of those coached by Auld at Easter Road and was later bought by him when Bertie moved on to manage Partick Thistle. Higgins, an articulate defender of players' rights, also holds the firm opinion that Bertie was wrongly maligned as a manager and could, in fact, have gone on to become one of the great members of that profession had it not been for a regrettable twist of fate.

'The image Bertie had was unfair because in the years he was in charge at Firhill, Partick Thistle were as entertaining as any side in the Premier League when they played at home. It was when they moved outside of Maryhill that Bertie had misgivings about the quality of his team and decided to play a

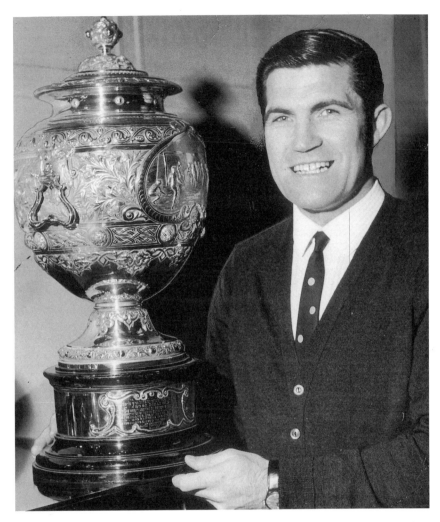

Bertie — A special relationship with Celtic that led to moments like this.

game of containment. Behind the bunnet like a small umbrella and the ridiculous cigars, though, there was a sound tactician at work. He was also a strict disciplinarian of the old school, mixing the influenes of Stein and Turnbull, but obviously not one without a sense of humour. Bertie was the original Glasgow patter merchant.

'There was the time when Partick Thistle were on their way to a goalless draw with Aberdeen at Firhill and Bertie decided to pull off Alex O'Hara. As Alex shuffled his way to the tunnel, as substitutes are wont to do, Bertie turned to his assistant, Pat Quinn, in the dug-out and without removing the cigar from his mouth said, "Look at him. He's so lifeless even the lice are jumpin' aff his heid!" '

It was not unknown, either, for Bertie to brandish his European Cup winners medal, which he wore on a chain round his neck, in front of players with whom he was determined to have the last word and say, 'Have you got one of these?' Lack of proper respect was never tolerated, as Jim Melrose, later to join Celtic, found out when he was taken off during a game in which Partick Thistle had already committed both substitutes. Melrose had responded to an instruction from the bench by using the phrase which has 'off' as its second word. Playing with ten men, Partick Thistle extended a one-goal lead to two goals and Bertie told a receptive, but not gullible audience of pressmen afterwards that it was an idea he felt had worked well enough before to give it a second try! Such was Bertie's charisma, Tony Higgins maintains he has yet to come across anyone who played under him who has a negative word to say about his ability. Those examples of Bertie's peerless phrases which cannot lend themselves easily to print have been expertly turned into an immensely enjoyable after-dinner speaking routine by Higgins but, behind his respectfully funny tribute, there lies one personal regret about Auld's managerial career.

'When he left Firhill to manage Hibs, Bertie was approaching the peak of his powers and found, in Tom Hart, who was then chairman at Easter Road, a kindred spirit.

'Tom was more than just a wealthy man in charge of a football club. He was also a committed fan who was willing to spend his money on improving the side he had always supported. Hibs could, under those circumstances, have gone on to become the most prominent side in the country outside of the Old Firm except that Tom Hart died and his successor, Kenny Waugh, was not on the same wavelength as Bertie. There then followed the inevitable parting of the ways.'

Auld was a firm believer in the manager's absolute right to

manage. Tom Hart had, in the early days of their relationship, come into his office one morning with a briefcase containing papers and cheques, reeling off a list of new players he felt it was imperative Hibs signed at the same time.

'Chairman, what colour is your hair?' came the response.

'White,' said Tom Hart.

'Why don't you let my hair go that colour, then, worrying about who we should buy?' said Bertie, bringing the conversation to a close.

The sense of potential never having been given the opportunity to be fully realised is strengthened by the unsatisfactorily meandering course of his managerial career thereafter. Bertie scuffled around the periphery of the game with Hamilton Accies and then endured a short and tempestuous association with Ken Bates, the chairman of Chelsea, when he bought over control of Partick Thistle during Bertie's second time at Firhill. What he perceived as interference from within brought to an end his time in charge of Dumbarton and has so far led to Bertie remaining on the outside looking in on a game that might be thought the poorer for his lack of professional involvement.

The years spent with Celtic remain the most cherished of his memories and affectionate recollection of them overcomes any bitterness he might feel about what happened anywhere else. There have, according to Bertie, been approaches to him to indulge in that brand of journalism which has personalities like him 'lift the lid' on big clubs like Celtic. They have all been given the same answer.

'As far as I'm concerned, I have had a special relationship with Celtic which goes back to 1955. If I did write anything, these people would be disappointed because it would be full of praise and respect for Celtic.'

Bertie Auld *International Appearances*

1959

May	Holland (a)	2-1
June	Portugal (a)	0-1
November	Wales (h)	1-1

CHAPTER 7

Bobby Lennox

IT IS DOUBTFUL IF THE HOUSTON ASTRODOME, IN Texas, was ever graced by a more decorated person, with the possible exception of any members of the U.S. shuttle programme who may have visited from the space centre that was the city's other, main distinguishing feature, than the Scottish footballer who stood to attention for the national anthem before the Houston Hurricanes played Dallas Tornadoes in 1978. Whatever else the fledgling game had going for it in America, there would have been few teams able to boast someone who had, in what might be called the real world, a record eleven league championship medals as well eight winners mementoes of the Scottish Cup. Five League Cup winners medals were also added to by the supreme distinction of being one of eleven Britons who first won the European Cup.

In his time, the man in question had become Celtic's top, post-war goalscorer and second only in the club's history of achievement in that direction behind the legendary Jimmy McGrory. Such was his prowess, he had once been runner-up to another of the game's names revered the world over, the Portuguese internationalist, Eusebio, for goals scored in a single season throughout the continent of Europe.

The greatly respected Manchester United and England internationalist, Bobby Charlton, whose testimony would have been readily accepted anywhere without the need for a preliminary oath to promise honesty, said this man could have extended his career by anything up to five years had they played in the same side together. Don Revie, an adversary when managing Leeds United, had once been moved to say to Jock Stein that his player was the best blind side runner he had ever seen on the football pitch anywhere in the world. Carrying credentials like those, and the recognition of his services to Celtic that came with the award of the M.B.E. from the Queen, into the environment of an American league in which dedication was, in some cases, less than fanatical might have coaxed the established celebrity to consider that he had done his bit and was being paid to give what amounted to an elaborate curtain call.

When the person in question put his right hand over his heart and gave a spirited rendition of the 'Star Bangled Banner', therefore, one of his native-born team-mates could not resist asking how such emotion could be put into something that was supposed to inspire others.

'Because I'm taking your money,' was the answer.

Bobby Lennox knew of no other way to play the game than with the intention of giving an honest day's work for whoever employed him and regardless of whether it was for pounds and pence or dollars and cents . . . .

Bobby Lennox made his birthplace of Saltcoats, on the Ayrshire coast, famous for something other than buckets and spades in what was once the holiday haven of the West of Scotland's working class. It would, though, be impossible to meet anybody with a less complicated view of how he was able to sustain such brilliance than the one who is now on the coaching staff at Celtic Park after nineteen years of meritorious service on the park. Bobby has gone round the world and back again in Celtic's employ, broadening his horizons but never losing touch with his roots. Today, he still lives in Saltcoats and has, much to his delight, now gone full

The young Lennox in an old, familiar goalscoring pose.

circle by playing his football for recreation in the municipal parks of the town.

'I started off playing for fun in the park before getting into organised football at amateur, junior, senior and, ultimately, international level. Now, I play in friendly matches for the team which represents the pub I own in Saltcoats. The enjoyment is as familiar as the surroundings. For me, football was a great job that I didn't want to lose. It also enabled me to get paid for something I would have done for nothing.

'The game never drove me to despair or caused me to feel

weighed down by the pressure that was felt by others. Perhaps I was lucky in respect of the fact that I was absolutely content living in a place like Saltcoats, where I was never treated like Bobby Lennox of Celtic but as wee Bobby from Quay Street, a two-story tenement one hundred yards or so from the harbour.'

Lennox's sunny disposition matched his surroundings and that was vouched for by the remarkable disciplinary statistic of only one booking in almost two decades in a domestic context and that for an alleged offence against Clyde at Shawfield which he still regards to this day as an unnecessary blemish on an otherwise pristine record.

'I had my hands on the ball and so did a Clyde defender. We were both in the middle of contesting who was due a throw-in when Clyde's Willie McVie, a sizeable character, knocked both of us on to the adjoining dog track. It was then the referee arrived and the crowd shared my disbelief when he produced his book to take my name.'

It was Jock Stein, who was proud of the fact that Lennox had never made an enemy in the game, who had instilled in him the realisation that he possessed the weapons which could inflict the most hurtful form of retaliation on opponents. The player's speed and strength brought him 297 competitive goals in all for Celtic and Stein would have been entitled to take a lot of the credit for that since he was the one who transformed a career that was waning almost before it had properly started by keeping Lennox at the club when he was on the verge of being sold to Falkirk.

'Big Jock was the first to see that my potential was not in being an orthodox winger but in using my assets in a more forceful way through the middle. Before then, though, Celtic had used me as an outside right, a position I had never played, and my progress was so unconvincing I wondered if I was going to make it at all. Those were dark days for the club. I remember my first goal coming in a league match against Third Lanark at home in 1963. It was the second of four Celtic scored

Lennox and the sunny disposition from Saltcoats.

in the opening quarter of an hour in that game, and yet we still managed not to win because Third Lanark had equalised with forty minutes of the game left to play! That was one of six appearances I made in my first season but it was another, against Third Lanark in the Glasgow Cup final, which gave me my first medal for the club and I cherished it greatly because there seemed no guarantee then of there being any more to come. It was also my good fortune to have a strong end to the season in the reserve side and I felt the impression created had been strong enough to help the club keep faith with me. However, when the players heard the following season that Jock Stein was returning to the club, my first instinct was to think that my time was up and since Falkirk had been one of those clubs who were interested in me while I was playing junior football with Ardeer Recreation I took the rumours of their approach for me very seriously.'

Stein, though, knew he was looking at the model of professionalism as coveted by any manager. Lennox was a dedicated trainer who, when the day's work was over at Celtic Park, would push himself just as hard on the beach near his home in the afternoons. In Bobby's estimation, there was not a season spent with Celtic when he could not have gone into a fully competitive match with complete confidence two days after pre-season training had started. Staying in the healthy enviroment of Saltcoats and having a steady girlfriend (Kathryn, later to become Mrs Lennox) was also Jock's idea of the perfect recipe for longevity in a player's career.

The fact that Bobby was not as celebrated as the more flamboyant players at Celtic Park, like Jimmy Johnstone, Bertie Auld and Tommy Gemmell, actually pleased Stein, too, since less publicity meant more freedom from opponents who were remiss enough not to notice that Lennox was invariably at the end of the others' good work.

'A lot was made of my pace but it was also possible to beat a marker by the quickness of thought that can buy you a head start. My only source of frustration was that I could be too quick for referees and linesmen when marginal decisions had to be made. There was one game against Dundee United where I scored four times and only one of them was allowed to stand. What's more it was the fourth attempt but, fortunately, it turned out to be the only goal of the game. That kind of thing never got me down too much, though, because my philosophy was that once a game was over it was only worth bothering about if it made you all the more determined to try harder the next time in the event of a defeat. Besides which, it was necessary to have your wits about you at all times under Jock Stein's management. Once we had won the Scottish Cup against Dunfermline, months after his arrival, it might have been thought that we could have gone into our next game, which was also the last of the season, and been forgiven anything. Big Jock went mad, though, because we lost to a Dunfermline team who were, not unnaturally, out for quick revenge. They won 5-1 and the cup might as well have been won by somebody else as Jock went through the card in his condemnation of us. The experience also taught me to sit still when he was in a foul temper. Mistakenly, I had decided to move in the general direction of the bath when Jock paused for breath, but he was only inhaling in preparation for a fresh onslaught.

'Where do you think you're going? Don't move until I'm finished,' he said.

'It was a lesson in what kind of standard we had set ourselves and how anything which fell beneath that level would not be tolerated under any circumstances. The team did not have to be reminded too often, though. There was a productive innocence about Celtic in those days which stemmed from all of us having known what it was like to earn our living from ordinary jobs before we got into professional football and actually enjoying being in each others' company. There was a tour of America organised after we had won Celtic the club's first league championship for twelve years, in 1966. We were to be away from home for five weeks and play nine matches, which would have been the cause of a dressing-room mutiny at some places. All I can recall is the players gathering round at Celtic Park and reading the itinerary out loud, occasionally shouting things like, "Look, we're going to San Francisco!" Visiting places like that and getting paid for the privilege seemed like a great idea to us.'

The serious aspect of the trip was not overlooked and it was while in the United States that the understanding was forged between Bobby Lennox and Bertie Auld. The latter would return hom able to summarise his partner's willingness to work in a typically graphic phrase: 'Wee Bobby? He'd chase paper on a windy day!'

There was no wind on 25 May, 1967 when the European Cup was won against Inter Milan or when the result was followed up by Lennox scoring the goal that beat Real Madrid in their own Bernabeau Stadium during Alfredo di Stefano's testimonial match. Only optimism breezed through Celtic's squad, and Bobby in particular. Jimmy Johnstone, from whom he had become an inseparable friend, swore that having been brought up in Saltcoats had given Lennox stronger lungs than any other player at Celtic Park, though that might have been his defence against the obvious comparisons which could have been made about the contrasting lifestyles of two otherwise perfectly compatible personalities.

They shared a liking for the same type of music and humour as well as an aversion to taking life too seriously, except when it came to maintaining Celtic's domestic supremacy at the expense of a Rangers side who always had to be viewed as the ultimate threat to that authority. There was one day, though, when Johnstone refused to accept that his friend's pursuit of victory at Ibrox was as committed as his own.

'I had narrowly missed a couple of chances in the first half but Jimmy was obviously not in the mood for accepting that they can't go in all of the time. As the teams went down the tunnel at half time, I was suddenly jumped on from behind. It wasn't a Rangers player, though, it was Jimmy with his hands around my neck and snarling, ''are you ******* trying not to score?'' We won the game in the end, of course, and I got one of the three goals we scored. Wee Jimmy planted a big kiss on my cheek when that one went in. That was just the way he was.'

Games against Rangers were loved by Lennox because they brought out the best in him and for reasons that had nothing to do with sectarianism. Jock Stein knew this to be an irrefutable statement of fact as well and once compromised his own managerial approach to team selection in order to accommodate the singular talent at his disposal.

'The big man once told me that I would be playing for the reserve side in their derby with Rangers. On the Saturday

Lennox — Perpetual motion.

morning, he called my house while I was still in bed and asked me what I had been doing the night before. He must have known without waiting for my reply that I would never have deviated from my normal, pre-match routine of getting to bed by nine o'clock on a Friday night, reserve team or otherwise. All he really wanted to say was that he had had a change of mind and that I would be playing for the first team at Ibrox.

My last words to him on the telephone were, if I remember correctly, "Ya beauty!" '

'When I came off from speaking to big Jock, I had this mental image of him lying in bed the night before, unable to sleep and thinking to himself, 'That wee so and so always does well against Rangers at Ibrox. They know that. I know that. He knows that . . .' In any event, I had a serviceable game and forced John Greig into the mistake that allowed Willie Wallace to score the first of the two goals that won the points.'

Wallace, who had come from Hearts, was one of a succession of forwards brought to the club by Stein without demur from Lennox, whose job security was what was under threat after all.

'I accepted that it was better to have a large squad to choose from and that it was up to me to make sure I kept my place. The idea of asking for a transfer never crossed my mind because I tried it once and the nervous energy I used up then was worse than all my playing years put together. It was the season after every domestic and European trophy had been won, 1967/68, and we had been drawn against Dunfermline in the Scottish Cup at Celtic Park. When I got to the ground, I discovered to my disbelief that I had been left out. To make matters worse, Celtic lost and I went home and told my dad that I was going to ask away. He was unhappy about the idea but when I arrived at Celtic Park on the following Monday morning I got out of the car with my farewell speech in my head. On the way to Jock's office, I suffered a sudden loss of memory! By Tuesday, I had decided it was the kind of thing best done on a Wednesday and so it went on until the Friday, when I happened to be passing the manager's office and he called me inside. The boss could tell I had not been my usual, carefree self and without waiting for the explanation told me that he had left me out against Dunfermline because he honestly felt I could be rested and that any eleven players in green and white hoops would intimidate the other side. Jock then broke the habit of a lifetime and told me I was in the team for the following day.

"The next morning, I got up with a huge weight lifted from my shoulders, scored two of the goals that beat Partick Thistle and Bobby Lennox's unspoken revolt at Celtic Park was over. I knew that some of the major clubs in England would have taken me in a minute because whenever I had been in the company of players from Spurs and Everton, for example, they had told me how highly rated I was by the managers of their clubs. That kind of talk never unsettled me, though, and I wasn't upset when, years after the event, I discovered by accident that Bertie Mee, while he was in charge of Arsenal, had offered what was then a British record transfer fee for me. Big Jock never mentioned a word about it but it didn't matter, because, at the age of 15, I had spent four days in London with Chelsea as a trialist and I cried from the moment I left Saltcoats until I got back home again. Apart from having no desire to live away from where I felt most comfortable, I didn't want to play for anybody but Celtic.'

If Stein had taken the pragmatic view that what Lennox didn't know wouldn't hurt him at the time of Arsenal's interest, there existed between the two men a reciprocal honesty that was evident in all other matters and which the manager was not afraid to demonstrate in public. On one occasion, Lennox was out through injury and beginning the road back to recovery with a lung-searing training session under Stein's supervision at Celtic Park. Having been told to come back for more of the same in the afternoon, Bobby repaired to a hotel on the South side of Glasgow for a midday meal that was interrupted by a telephone call from Stein.

'His first question was to ask me if I had a tie on, knowing full well that I didn't because there was no reason for me to be dressed in a formal manner. Being meticulous about that kind of thing, Jock told me to go home and get one before coming back and playing for the reserve side against Ayr United that evening.

'I played for the first hour and scored before being substituted. As I passed through the tunnel into the corridor that led to the home team's dressing room door, the gaffer was coming down the stairs from the directors' box and shook me warmly by the hand while complimenting me on my performance. He told me that other players at the height of their profession, which I was by then, might not have given such earnest effort under the same difficulties and thanked me for my honesty. He was a big fox, Jock, but when he spoke to you like that it left you feeling ten feet tall.'

The figure ten enters Lennox's story in a less positive fashion, since it represents the number of full international caps he won for Scotland, all of them gained in a brief, four-year period between 1966 and 1970 in the midst of a career that was characterised by its productivity and longevity. Bobby also scored in his first two internationals and it was the second of those, against the reigning World Champions, England, at Wembley, which provided him with his personal highlight of the time spent playing in dark blue.

'My dad wasn't fanatical about football but as the bus carrying the Scotland team made its way up the famous Wembley Way I saw him, clear as a bell, sitting on the steps outside the stadium wearing his good coat and looking as pleased as could be. When I scored one of the goals in our 3-2 win, my first thought was for my dad and I got a glow of satisfaction all over me. The funny thing was that, while he wasn't obsessed by football, his youngest boy was, for the son of a bookmaker, totally uninterested in horseracing and couldn't have backed a winner to save himself. My dad was the nicest man in the world and gave me a terrific family life that was free of problems and allowed me to concentrate on the day when I would become a professional footballer.

'I never got upset over having only ten caps, either, because there were a lot of terrific players about then and competition for places was always fierce. It was exactly the same at Celtic Park, and though it will sound like sacrilege to the modern thinkers on the game, I would scrap the Premier League and go back to the old, two-league system to help re-

Lennox in the act of proving how he became Celtic's top post-war goalscorer.

create that kind of rivalry for places. It is virtually impossible now for managers to introduce youngsters because they always have to live with the consequences if anything goes wrong, there being no such thing as a meaningless match in the Top Ten and the league being full of players who were bought for huge fees in an atmosphere of intense need to get success as quickly as possible. Extending the major league to 18 clubs once again might appal some people but it would provide those fixtures in which a club's promising talent could be allowed free expression. As a coach at Celtic Park, I know there are exciting prospects anxious to emerge. Equally, I know why Billy McNeill can't bring them in at will.'

Lennox came perilously close to being completely serious for a moment and letting the laugh lines that crease his face recede when assembling his thoughts on the subject of coaching as opposed to playing.

'The playing days were the best and coaching doesn't begin to compensate for their passing, that's for sure. I know that I could have gone on for another two years at the top had

it not been for a serious injury, and even when I became coach
to the reserve side I still thought I was one of the players. I kept
following the team out on to the park before their games until
the goalkeeper, Peter Latchford, said to me one day, "Bobby,
what are you doing here? You're supposed to be in the dug-
out!" I played the game for enjoyment and because I loved
Celtic. It had nothing to do with the money.'

Similar sentiments to those have, over the years, been
expressed by a variety of players at Celtic Park whose tongues
were ultimately shown to have been firmly imbedded in their
cheeks at the time of speaking. Lennox, though, would put his
money where his mouth was in 1978 when, after Billy McNeill
succeeded Jock Stein as manager, he agreed to go back to the
club from America for an unspecified amount, and without a
signing-on fee, when he could have had that inducement as well
as a contract for a fixed period from Kilmarnock or Ayr
United. By then, he had also, at the age of 33, survived a
broken leg that would at least have implanted the idea of retiral
in the mind of many another player at what is popularly known
as the veteran stage.

The incident happened at Ibrox after a collision with
Rangers captain, John Greig. There was never any question of
animosity as Lennox, typically, responded by saying it was the
first time Greig had ever caught him and that since he had been
bothered by ankle trouble which had never had time to heal
properly, a few weeks in plaster was actually good remedial
therapy. It was also symptomatic of the relationship which
existed between player and manager that Lennox told Stein he
would only return to Celtic Park when he was fully fit and then
spent weeks working in a public park and on the soft sand of
Stevenston.

After seventeen years of playing for Celtic, the majority of
them spent under Stein, it was an understandably emotional
time when the partnership was broken up in March, 1978. The
words 'freed' or 'released' were never mentioned in the
conversations which sorted out the details of the move to

Celtic got everything Lennox had to offer.

Houston but Bobby left the ground for what he thought was the last time emotionally numbed. Stein, in turn, showed the depth of his feeling by turning up, wrongly as it turned out, at Prestwick Airport to say farewell to his player. A quick telephone call to Glasgow Airport briefly re-united the men the morning after Bobby had worn a Celtic jersey for the last time under Stein and marked the occasion by scoring two goals, one of them the equaliser, as the reserve side came from being three goals down to draw with Motherwell.

Celtic, under the old or the new order, got everything Lennox had to offer all times. Enthusiasm being his main character trait, Bobby, whose musical hero was Elvis Presley, sent Stein a postcard from the singer's mansion in Memphis, Gracelands, to say that, having got there, he had achieved all that was left to him. The message may have been heartfelt but it would also turn out to be inaccurate, since Bobby returned to Scotland to win a league championship medal and a record-breaking eighth Scottish Cup winners medal in what really was his final game in Celtic's first team, when Rangers were defeated at Hampden in May, 1980.

'If I had known the Cup Final was going to be my last game, I would probably have shot myself. When the end did come, it felt like a fatal blow, in any case. I had been attempting to instruct a young reserve on the art of crossing the ball when I suffered a terrible pain in the area of my groin. There was pain and awful discoloration and when I visited Dr Abrami at the Victoria Infirmary in Glasgow one day he told me my career was over. It was the day another of my heroes, Steve McQueen, died and it was a miserable time for me.

'A few weeks before the bad news was delivered, though, I had gone to Holyrood Palace to receive the M.B.E. for services to Celtic, as it said on the citation. It was a day I could never forget and what sticks in my mind is that the person in the queue in front of me to meet the Queen was someone from Saltcoats who had been in the year ahead of me at St. Michael's school, Thomas Lafferty, whose good work had been done in the oil industry. When I got home that night and took off the top hat and tails to exchange them for denims and training shoes, I put my feet up and opened a can of lager. In your moments of serene contemplation like that, all your blessings are able to be counted properly, and since Celtic filled me with those while promising more to come I realised it was not possible to ask for any more out of life.'

Bobby Lennox *International Appearances*

1966

November	Northern Ireland (h)	2-1

1967

April	England (a)	3-2
May	U.S.S.R. (h)	0-2
November	Wales (h)	3-2

1968

February	England (h)	1-1
October	Denmark (a)	1-0
December	Cyprus (a)	5-0

1969

April	West Germany (h)	1-1

1970

April	Wales (h)	0-0

CHAPTER 8

Charlie Nicholas

THERE ARE THOSE WHO WOULD DISPUTE Charlie Nicholas' entitlement to be considered among the outstanding names in Celtic's history. They would contend that such a distinction can only be earned over a long number of years, consistency while withstanding the peculiar pressures of a job with the Old Firm being the main criterion that has to be fulfilled. Between September, 1981 and May, 1983, Charlie played one hundred games from the start under the manager-ship of Billy McNeill, coming on in another nine as substitute. In that time a total of eighty goals were put against the name of Nicholas, all of them contributing towards a legend that did not diminish long after he had left Celtic Park. The player who began the '80s by establishing himself in the affections of supporters who could see their own image being reflected in his appearance ended that same decade by taking part in a display of mutual appreciation which vouched for his status in the eyes of those not given to error of judgement when assessing who has properly enhanced the hoops.

Nicholas, visiting Celtic Park as an Aberdeen player, was taken off late in a game that was crucial to the championship aspirations of both clubs. As Charlie ambled towards the dug-out, an outpouring of warmth came, presumably to the astonishment of Aberdeen's travelling support, from all corners of the ground. As remarkable was Charlie's reflex

100

gesture of recognition, clapping his hands in reciprocal respect before dipping his head out of sight while the ovation went on. It was an incident which made its own statement: Charlie was still the crowd's favourite and he had never lost his regard for them . . . .

The middle child of Chic and Rena, Nicholas was born in Glasgow's Maryhill, fertile territory for Celtic in respect of finding players and acquiring supporters for what is correctly known as the east terracing, coloquially defined as the 'Celtic end', during every home game.

The adolescent Nicholas can also recall association with the club once reaching such heights of excitement that during a penalty kick decider against Rangers in the Drybrough Cup final of 1974 he had clung to his father to help stop himself shaking, only to find his guardian had developed an involuntary tremble of his own that was finally granted respite when Jimmy Johnstone settled the issue with the last kick of the game.

From a close-knit family, Charlie thought of himself as being an affectionate child but also shy and withdrawn at St. Gregory's Primary School, where his natural talent with a ball was the most eloquent way he could express himself.

'The daft thing was that the teachers more or less left it up to me to pick the school team. What was even sillier was that I played as a sweeper in those days. I kept that position when I moved on to St. Columba of Iona Secondary School and my progress was good enough to draw attention to myself. The first team to show an interest in me was, believe it or not, Rangers Boys' Club, though I would have to make it a matter of public record that I never did wear the blue jersey. For some reason that boys' club wore white shirts, which suited me because I was quite a biased little chap then and couldn't have brought myself to wear those colours. As it was, I never told my family or friends where I was going when I was taken out to the Drumchapel housing scheme one Saturday morning to make my Rangers debut. The strain couldn't have had an over-whelming effect, because I was eventually asked for my particulars by a Rangers scout. It was, though, still in the less enlightened days when the mere mention of St. Columba of Iona was an impediment to the discussion being taken any further, for which I was as grateful as anybody. It was my late uncle, Tommy, who pointed me in the right direction by taking me along to trials that were being held by Celtic Boys' Club in the East end of Glasgow.

'There were young hopefuls everywhere, of course, and my introverted nature was about to get the better of me when I decided on an impulse to disobey everything I had been taught by my parents and tell a lie. All those in front of me were answering "inside left" when they were asked to stipulate their best position. Anxiety to get a foot on the Celtic ladder made me say "inside right", and it was enough to get me a trial and acceptance into the Boys' Club at the age of thirteen. There-after, though, I got the distinct impression I was never going to make it all the way at Celtic Park.'

The hesitancy on the part of those who guided youngsters through their development on Celtic's behalf was not shared by others, however, most notably in England. A trip to Ipswich Town, then still managed by Bobby Robson, was followed by the offer of £4,000 to sign that was only turned down because of a slavish adherence to the Celtic cause and the imperishable hope that he would graduate to Celtic Park one day. The greatest act of selflessness, though, involved a stay with Wolves, who offered the young Charlie terms that would have turned the head of many a boy and his parents.

'Sammy Chung was the manager at Molineaux then and he was so keen to get me he offered my dad £20,000 for my signature, At the time, my dad had been made redundant from his job as a printer on the *Daily Express* when they closed down their plant in Glasgow and it was an extreme hardship for him to keep me in football boots, never mind turn down a windfall like that. He shared my dreams of Celtic, though, and that

Charlie scores against Rangers in an Old Firm encounter.

made it easy to resist the temptation. I left school without an 'O' level to my name because the pursuit of my ambition had distracted me from exams, and the first contribution I made to the family housekeeping came when I went to work as an apprentice mechanic in a garage that was owned by a pal of Billy McNeill's called Tommy Coakley.'

By then, Charlie's career had been put on a steadier footing by Frank Cairney, a man responsible for shaping the future of many who made Celtic's first team from uncertain beginnings, and who was intrigued by a player who scored so frequently while not playing in a forward role. A move to what was obviously his natural position brought the expected results for Charlie and at a time which happily coincided with Billy McNeill leaving Aberdeen and taking over as Celtic manager in 1978.

'The first time I met him I was so overawed I couldn't get out the words, even though Billy was asking me to come into Celtic Park and work for two weeks on a full-time basis. Previously, I used to arrive in the evenings with grease still on my face and hands, and to say I enjoyed the change that allowed me to train with players I was still cheering from the terracing is an understatement. In that respect, I wasn't alone, either. After I signed for Celtic, and took my weekly wage from £18 to £30, I was still a supporter as well as a member of the groundstaff. At the end of Billy's first season, as everyone will remember, Celtic won the championship by beating Rangers 4-2 on our own ground in what was, for us, the last game of our programme. I was one of those who cleaned out the home dressing room and laid out the kit on that unforgettable night of 21 May, 1979. There was myself, Danny Crainie, Willie McStay, Gerry Crawley and 'Shanty' Ferrie, all of us suddenly overcome by the dramatic nature of the occasion. Consequently, the laundry room was raided for five extra stips that were smuggled out and taken to my mother's house. That night, Charlie Nicholas took his place in the 'jungle' and became the original supporter with a strip. I'll never forget Danny McGrain leading the team on a lap of honour and being as excited as everybody else until I saw Neilly Mochan, who was responsible for the team's kit, coming too close to the fans for comfort. Nicholas, McStay and the rest were then to be found hiding behind the perimeter wall before going home to get the strips washed, ironed and replaced without detection.'

Getting a jersey of his own, and a peg to hang it on in the first-team dressing room, was a privilege that would, and could, not be denied Charlie much longer. His reserve-team début came the following season and saw him score twice against Hibs. On 6 September, 1980, he started in the first team by scoring in each of his first nine league and cup matches. The reaction was as predictable as his threat in front of goal.

'The ultimate accolade came when the local branch of the Orange Order started to re-route the traditional marches made by their band so that they came past my parents' door, which was encircled by what seemed like every Celtic supporter in the neighbourhood. That apart, there was a more serious, emotional drain that came with the excitement of making a

Charlie says goodbye to the Celtic support first time round.

name for myself so quickly. People like Danny McGrain, Tommy Burns and Davie Provan recognised the symptoms and did their bit to help. Danny was the biggest name at the club but he used to take me to his house in the afternoon, show me videos of Celtic games and offer me the benefit of his wisdom. The other two were well known for the manner in which they went out of their way to assist the youngsters at Celtic Park. That's why it was laughable that I should have been stuck with the 'good time Charlie' image at that time. I couldn't have gone out to the local pubs even if I'd wanted to, and when I did venture across the doorstep it was to meet Willie McStay and Danny Crainie in the City centre and be back home on the last bus. It would be some playboy who had a transcard! I came from a Celtic-minded family, don't forget, and the preservation of my career there took precedence over all else. I was still a long way off thinking I was the finished article. My first appearance in an Old Firm game, for instance, was a disaster as Celtic lost and I was substituted by the late Johnny Doyle. My knees had been knocking together so badly at Ibrox,

I was having difficulty kicking the ball properly at the warm-up which took place half an hour before the kick-off.

'The next time, though, I went out to prepare with some words of advice from George McCluskey to help me. In order to blank out the atmosphere, George suggested I should sing to myself, so I ran around the park belting out "Hail, Hail, the Celts are here!" It must have worked, too, because I scored twice, Celtic won and from then on we remained unbeaten on the way to winning the title. If I had to isolate highlights from my time as a Celtic player, that first season, with its 39 appearances from the start and another 6 as a substitute, would have to be the main one. It spawned my partnership with Frank McGarvey, for one thing, and nobody has to tell me how much I owed him during my time at Celtic Park for the way he helped set up so many goals for me.'

There was still no guarantee, however, of a regular place in the first team so long as Billy McNeill was obliged to find an answer to the arithmetical impossibility of trying to make three — Nicholas, McGarvey and McCluskey — go into the only two places he had available in attack. It was during a time of uncertainty, in fact, that Charlie found himself playing for the reserve side at Greenock against Morton on 18 January, 1982 and suffered the broken leg which would clear up far quicker than the doubts it instilled in his mind about the future. An unintentional collision with Joe McLaughlin, partly caused by wintry conditions, is remembered by Charlie for a variety of reasons; there being no ambulance available at Cappielow, which meant he had to suffer in the dressing room while feeling faint and being looked after by Davie Provan. Eventually, he was driven to hospital by Celtic's doctor, John Fitzsimmons, a deeply religious man whose concern for the condition of the prized cargo he was carrying was such that he said the rosary out loud on the way from the ground. The diagnosis being as bad as was feared, Nicholas was suddenly given cause to reflect on how precarious a lifestyle it was playing at the highest level.

'Gone were the chants of 'Charlie, Charlie' from the

The last goal for Celtic during his first stay.

crowd and the backslapping that went on in the street. I was proud of myself, though, for the way I dedicated myself to a quick recovery and one that was so complete the following season had a dream-like quality. Scoring 46 goals in all competitions for Celtic, however, only brought me to the point where I formed the conclusion that would be the basic source of a disagreement destined to take me away from the club. Quite simply, I thought I had done enough in the two and a half years that had gone before to merit becoming as well paid as the highest wage earner on the staff. I would have settled for parity, you'll notice, but I think that the club had by then got into the dangerous way of thinking that there were certain players who, because of their background, would wear the jersey for nothing. I was as naive as the next youngster at one stage in my life in thinking that I would have done that, too. I was living with my mother then, though, and probably thought you could live on nothing but love of the jersey.

Nicholas, during the season when his goals for Scotland took his total to 53, was working on a contract that was worth a basic £85 a week, rising to a maximum of £226. Celtic's first attempt to amend those terms would have taken him up to £300, their final compromise being £400 with a £20,000 signing-on-fee for a four-year contract. In retrospect, Charlie now knows he made a dreadful mistake in refusing the offer but his earnest belief at the time was that the issue was as much about principle as money. Billy McNeill was helpless when trying to resolve the problem with the board and it was during a trip to Ireland that Charlie told him there was no other recourse but to move elsewhere. Between then and leaving for Arsenal, there was only one day when the player was given cause to think about a change of mind.

'On the final day of the 1982/83 season, Celtic played Rangers at Ibrox, theoretically still having a chance of beating Dundee United to the League championship. We were two goals down at half-time but Tom McAdam, Frank McGarvey and myself got the score to 4-2 in our favour with five minutes left to play. There were banners draped over the Celtic end of the ground saying 'Charlie, don't go' and the crowd were calling for me, so much so that I became badly affected by the whole atmosphere and spent from then until the final whistle running around with tears in my eyes and pretending it was as a result of the strong sunshine. The experience troubled me so much I left Ibrox that night preoccupied and silent. Instead of meeting some of the other players in a pub that was our usual haunt after a match, I went home and locked myself indoors for fully forty-eight hours. It was then I thought about giving in and re-signing for Celtic. The only way I can prove the whole episode wasn't entirely about money is to say that, with the help of foreign agents, I could have gone to any of eight clubs on the Continent who would have paid me more than the one I eventually joined, Arsenal.

'All I can add is that I made the wrong decision. I knew it soon after I went to London and I paid the price for it by having Arsenal take away from me some of the God-given talent with which I was blessed. What I should have done, if I

Jim Leighton foils Charlie this time.

hadn't stayed with Celtic, was sign for Liverpool. I was highly impressed by their manager, Joe Fagan, but I took fright over being the odd man out behind Kenny Dalglish and Ian Rush and finding myself in the Anfield reserve team.'

An even more obvious move might have been to join Manchester United, a club whose supporters share an affinity with those of Celtic and would have idolised Charlie. A meeting with Ron Atkinson, then Old Trafford manager, during which the latter spoke more about himself than the team, had an unsettling effect on Charlie, though, and a marriage apparently made in Heaven never reached the altar.

London is not the most forgiving of places for those who have fallen down on their luck, as Charlie then found out. The Highbury playing staff had no other Scots with whom he could mix, and the obsessive attentions of the tabloid press became an irritation, particularly when photographs printed (normally on a Saturday morning) of Charlie in female company usually featured him with his sister, Janice, a regular visitor to keep him company.

'On the field I knew the extent of the mistake I had made at the end of my first season at Highbury. It would have been better to hold up my hands there and then and move on but, unwisely, I stuck it out in spite of the fact that Arsenal were draining out of me the arrogance that was central to my style of play. The lowest point came when our coach, Don Howe, played me as Bryan Robson's marker against Manchester United at Old Trafford. The result was a totally predictable 4-0 win for the home team. My strength was in receiving the ball with my back to goal, turning and running at defences, not trying to nullify one of the best players in Britain.'

In four years at Highbury, the sum total of Charlie's achievement was a win over Liverpool in the final of the Littlewoods Cup that was decided by his winning goal. The most distressing incident came when he revisited Celtic Park for a pre-season friendly and was verbally turned on by the same supporters who had once idolised him.

'They thought I had committed treason by leaving the club. That didn't affect me but I did feel for the members of my family and those of my girlfriend (now my wife's) family, who are all Celtic through and through, but were made to squirm in their stand seats. I could rationalise what happened because when Kenny Dalglish left Celtic years earlier I had been one of those who felt let down by him and stood in the jungle making my feelings known when he came back for the first time in a Liverpool jersey.'

Three years after the taunting of Charlie, the same supporters were consumed by the idea that he could have been on the verge of returning to Celtic. His contract with Arsenal was up for renewal and another pre-season visit to Glasgow had led to the bizarre sight of Nicholas scoring against his old team and then running half the length of the Jungle making apologetic signs. There has always been a widely held belief that Charlie actually turned down the offer to come back that had been made to him by Billy McNeill, himself restored to the job of manager after four years of similarly involuntary exile in England.

Charlie in aggressive mood.

'No-one can ever say I rejected Celtic. It's true I did meet Billy and terms were discussed, which excited me because Billy was the only manager who ever got the best out of me. The truth of the matter, though, is that I was never made a final offer by Celtic and so I signed on for another year with Arsenal.'

In the time that has elapsed since then, during which Charlie went to Aberdeen in December, 1988, what amounts to a crusade has been waged by Celtic supporters to have him brought back to the place where he started. It is something he has always been well aware of and for which he is truly grateful, since rejoining Celtic became the ruling passion in his life. In spite of the fact that he could never again be the lithe young man with long hair who left on a torrent of goals in 1983, and appreciates that it is a common trait for fans to turn to a former hero and invest their hopes in him when they feel let down by others, there is, he knows, an element who see him as a messianic figure. He doesn't kid himself either that he can ever rekindle what Arsenal put out.

'All I can say with honesty is that, first and foremost, it

would have been the major regret of my life if I hadn't got the opportunity to play for Celtic again before my career ended. The older I get, the stronger I find my passion for the club becoming once again. There were times at Pittodrie, for instance, when I ran about during games trying to find out Celtic's score somewhere else. When I applauded the Celtic fans as I was being substituted at Celtic Park it was because it would have been impolite to ignore their spontaneous show of affection for me. Now that I am back at the club as a player, I think the place and the people can lift me in a way that has been missing for years. I'm a different type of player now, but one who's still up to doing a specialised kind of job for Celtic.

'To sum up what has happened to me since 1983, I would have to be candid and say that my career never reached the heights it ought to have done or would have done if I'd stayed at Celtic Park. I should have signed the four-year contract when it was offered to me because I could then have learned my trade properly and, like Kenny Dalglish, realised my full potential at the same time before deciding what to do for the best. I don't think I ever had a really bad season at Arsenal or Aberdeen but I should have done better.

'Put it this way, it may be hard for outsiders to understand but I wanted to go back to Celtic because I know how good it can be when it is good at Celtic Park. There never was a day there when I didn't feel better for being a part of the club. If I was depressed, going inside Celtic Park cheered me up. Even if we lost, the ground had recuperative powers.

'I have this instinctive feeling that now is the ideal time of my life to return.

'It means so much to an awful lot of people who are dear to me. My father never took a complimentary ticket from me in all the time I was a Celtic player because he refused to desert his favourite place on the terracing. He hasn't seen anything like the same number of games since then but I know the old longing is back. My wife's family are involved in a Celtic supporters' club in Bannockburn and when she asks how "we"

Charlie turns away after scoring yet another goal for Celtic.

got on there is no doubt which team Claire is speaking about. I can only say I thought it my destiny to end up at Celtic Park and I hope I make them as happy as I am.'

Dreams come true and the prayers of many were answered when Charlie agreed to re-join Celtic. The person who was pleased most of all, of course, was Charlie himself.

'Deep down in my heart, I never thought the day would ever come when I would get the chance to go back. When you're young and sign for the club, it is like a dream but I have never experienced a feeling like the one I enjoyed when I took my wife to see me go back to what I consider to be home. I had known for a year that Billy McNeill was interested in getting me because he had told me so over a few drinks at the wedding of one of my former team-mates at Celtic Park, Davie Provan. The negotiations which went on later had nothing to do with money, either, but revolved around my misgivings about the Premier League, I don't think any side has suffered as much as

Celtic from the ever increasing hustle and bustle of the top ten. I had to consider whether I wanted to remain a part of that set up. Had it been any other club but Celtic, I think the answer would have been in the negative. At this point, anybody who wants to say I stayed in Scotland because I'm just a wee Celtic supporter is perfectly entitled to do so, because that is about as accurate a summation as it is possible to make.

'After seven years away, I decided that if I was ever going to regain some of the sharpness of my younger days then Celtic Park would be the only place to do it. I enjoy an obvious rapport with the crowd and Billy McNeill has always been able to motivate me in a way no other manager has done. Strange as it might sound, I'm also glad that I came back to the club having scored one of the goals that defeated Celtic in the Scottish Cup Final and kept them out of Europe.

'I should qualify that by saying I regret not having the chance to play in the Cup Winners Cup with Celtic. However, on a personal level, it was good for me to go back home with no suspicion attached to my name. As I walked towards the penalty spot that day at Hampden to face Packy Bonner, I knew two things. The first was that the balance of power during the penalty shoot-out had swung back in Celtic's favour and my kick was crucial for Aberdeen. Secondly, and as important, I could feel the knives of certain representatives of the media sharpening, ready for plunging in my back if I missed. I would have been remembered in a bad light even if Packy pulled off an unbelievable save as the one who cheated and deliberately missed against his favourite team. I could even see the headlines in my minds eye: ''Proper Charlie!'' Not only did I not want that stigma attached to my name but I can tell you now that I was so intent on being totally professional against Celtic that it had been agreed before the game that I would take any penalties for Aberdeen that came within the regulation ninety minutes.

'I have to be a more mature, responsible person than the one who used to play for Celtic. I'm married now and have a family, which means that I have come back to the club as a father figure in more senses than one. In the beginning, there was a naive wee chap who could get into trouble off the field sometimes. I don't think I was ever a bad boy but Glasgow could have its own particular pressures at that time. Celtic now have the older, wiser version of Charlie Nicholas. The crowd have a blind spot where I have been concerned in the past, but I honestly think they are now wise enough to know that they are not getting the player who left in 1983 but a more experienced individual aware of the team's needs. I will now be judged over the lifetime of my four year contract but everybody knows those will be the four happiest years of my career no matter what happens because Celtic have meant the world to me since childhood.'

Charlie Nicholas *International Appearances*

1983

March	Switzerland (h)	2-2
May	Northern Ireland (h)	0-0
June	England (a)	0-2
June	Canada (a)	2-0
June	Canada (a)	3-0
June	Canada (a)	2-0
October	Belgium (h)	1-1

1984

June	France (a)	0-2
September	Yugoslavia (h)	6-1
October	Iceland (h)	3-0

1985

February	Spain (a)	0-1
March	Wales (h)	0-1

1986

January	Israel (a)	1-0
March	Rumania (h)	3-0
April	England (a)	1-2
June	Denmark (a)	0-1
June	Uruguay (a)	0-0
September	Bulgaria (h)	0-0

1987

May	England (h)	0-0

1989

April	Cyprus (h)	2-1

CHAPTER 9

Tommy Burns

O N THE 16th OF DECEMBER, 1989, THE DAY OF his 33rd birthday, a player whose last game, ten days earlier, had been against the world renowned Ajax, of Amsterdam, found himself standing in the middle of a snowbound Fenwick Moor while emergency repairs were carried out on the bus taking Kilmarnock's team to play against East Fife at Bayview. It was the start of a day that would live in his memory as much as any in a career that had brought him six Premier League Championship medals, five Scottish Cup winners medals and one from the Skol Cup as well as eight international caps for Scotland. After the driver who was attempting to mend a faulty windscreen wiper had been knocked into the middle of the road by heavy gusts, narrowly avoiding being struck by a passing car, the team bus eventually spluttered its way as far as Coatbridge. When a replacement vehicle failed to turn up, it was decided that the by now bedraggled and sodden team members should travel in a fleet of taxis to Fife in order to fulfil their Second Division fixture. At five minutes to three, having mustered eleven players but with the substitutes yet to arrive, Kilmarnock were ordered to take the field on a playing surface that quickly became more treacherous than any the most famous player on it had ever experienced. By half-time the former inter-nationalist was shaking uncontrollably and confiding in his new team-mates that he felt as if he was going to die. Exhibiting the classic symptoms of hypothermia, it was only the instinct for self-preservation that carried him to the point where the referee finally conceded it was not a day for football and abandoned the match in spite of protests made, remarkably, by the home team. On the journey home, Tommy Burns sat back, closed his eyes and tried to take a philosophical point of view. What he had just been through represented the lowest point in his professional life and, as such, there was only one way his career in his new surroundings could go, and that was up . . . .

Tommy Burns was breaking in a new pair of boots at Bayview. His old ones had gone as presents to a couple of unsuspecting Celtic supporters who had been standing on the covered teracing known colloquially as the 'Jungle' on the night when an illustrious, eighteen-year-long affair came to an end against Dutchmen who must have wondered about the extravagant response when the substitutes boards were held up midway through the first half of a friendly match between the two famous clubs. Play was temporarily suspended while Tommy made a spontaneous run towards the area of the ground where he had stood as a boy and made his final, flamboyant gesture in front of its occupants. Symbolically, his boots were removed and given with the flourish of a matador to the crowd whose support had carried him through his time with the club. Barefoot, he took a slow, lingering farewell of Celtic Park and went back to the dressing room, where he was comforted by those who were sharing in the poignancy of the moment.

Tommy Burns' life has always been led as if it had been scripted beforehand instead of happening to turn out that way. Being born and brought up in Soho Street, which was located in that area of Glasgow defined only as the Calton and stood within walking distance of Celtic Park, Tommy had felt an emotional bond with the club that would dominate his adolescent and adult life. He had been educated by the Marist

Tommy and Roy Aitken when hair was long and time was short to make a name for yourself.

Brothers in St Mary's Primary School, the place where Celtic had been brought into being 67 years before he was born by a member of the same religious order, Brother Walfrid. The area was one of these in which the Kray twins would have gone about in threes and could have been described as rough and ready only by those looking for a euphemism. Petty crime was prevalent and gang violence was the other distinguishing feature. Tommy's recollections of both are understandably still vivid in his mind.

'At St Mary's school there was no such thing as a uniform and if you were smart you never wore the kind of clothes that were fashionable at the time. My outstanding memory is of the two boys who ignored that piece of wisdom and skipped a class to go out for cigarettes. When they came back to face the teacher they were both wearing underpants and nothing else because the rest had been removed from them at knifepoint. My type of homework at night was devising the route I could take home at four o'clock each day that would help me avoid the gang members from a rival part of the Calton. I would have to stress that I was never a member of any gang but there would not have been any time for a discussion on the subject had you been caught. I was short-sighted, too, and needed glasses but vanity used to prevent me from wearing them. So there were occasions when the bad guys had me by the throat before I knew they were there! The one thing I could see was the red mist descending when I lost the volcanic temper that had obviously come at birth with my red hair. One night, near my close in our tenement building, I was stopped by three boys who wanted my duffle coat and they weren't talking about having it on a loan basis, either! I was still hitting one of them when the other two were making good time in the opposite direction. That is nothing to be proud of but another indication of how hard a person had to work in order to survive, lessons which came in handy later.

'When the time came for me to leave school, I remember one of my teachers saying that, with a bit of effort, I could stay on and get some 'O' levels if I applied myself. I had to tell him that getting to the stage where I could get my third-year leaving certificate had taken its toll of my nerves and that I wanted out while I was still alive.'

Tommy's parents had split up when he was fifteen years old, though they remained on civilised terms, and his mother, who looked after him and his two sisters, Elizabeth and Anne, did not need to harbour any worries that there would be a gradual progression towards criminality after school had been completed. Used one night as an unwitting look-out man while some friends had carried out a close inspection of a van that was to deliver confectionary, the sight and sound of two Glasgow beat policemen had struck terror into his heart and

Tommy twists, Tommy turns.

convinced the teenage Tommy that it was time for him to dedicate himself to the opportunities that were opening up on the football field.

'I never felt that playing for Celtic was a way of escaping from anything, though. I am not ashamed to say I used to pray every night before I went to sleep that one day I would get the chance to play for the club who felt as if they were a part of my very being. My good fortune was in having about me in the parish of St. Mary's people who were adamant that I should be helped along the road. John Rice ran the Boys' Guild team that was affiliated to St. Mary's and once, when I was only eleven years old, he took me in his car straight up to the front door at Celtic Park and demanded to see Sean Fallon, who was then assistant manager to Jock Stein. Sean was out at the time but John left word with Jim Kennedy, a former Celtic player who was on the office staff, that I was to be signed by the club. Just like that, at the age of eleven! It was also John Rice who gave me my first pair of football boots and you can't forget kindness on that scale. Every day of my time with Celtic, I would drive past St. Mary's chapel, my old school and the pitch where the Boys' Guild played and be reminded of the people, like John, who helped me to achieve my greatest ambition.'

'Wee Tommy' Burns had his prayers answered in 1972 when he joined Celtic after having gone from Boys' Guild football to Eastercraigs, a Glasgow amateur side, and the Celtic Boys' Club. The size of the step he was about to take was enough to render the youngster so nervous that he turned down Celtic first of all after being overcome by his surroundings. Before leaving the ground, however, words of caution from his father ('D'ye know what you're doin', Thomas? This is Celtic, after all.'), forced Tommy to turn round and ask Celtic's scout, John Higgins, if he could take up the pen and the cause. A car and an address in Glasgow's stockbroker belt was still a long way off, though. As a schoolboy signing, Tommy was paid £5 a week in expenses. When he went on to the ground staff, that sum doubled: 'A little something extra for your mother,' as Sean Fallon summed up the increase. It was then time for the promising young player to come under the guidance of Jock Stein, whom he had idolised to the point of deification from the terracing.

'Big Jock had a beautiful smile and a vicious tongue, a tremendous sense of humour and a ferocious temper when he was roused. Our first fall-out, and my introduction to how hard it can be to make your way in this game, came one night before the reserve team left Celtic Park to play against Hamilton Accies. I wandered into the ground not expecting to get a game because the second team then tended to be the place for players who were temporarily out of the top side. I had turned up without a coat, however, and the big man took that to mean I had assumed I would be playing and not sitting in a draughty stand all night. Jumping to conclusions about his team selection was the one form of exercise Jock hated his players taking and he ordered Sean to give him the reserve-team sheet so that he could scribble something on it. To this day, I am convinced he was putting my name on the list and not

Determined to do well for Celtic.

taking it off, either to keep me warm or keep me wondering on
the bus trip to Lanarkshire if I would ever be forgiven for
allegedly taking my place for granted.

'In fact, I was earning £27 a week then and couldn't afford
to buy myself a coat. I was going out with a girl called
Rosemary Smith (later to be Mrs Burns) and had worn the
same brown suit for about two years. What with handing in
money to my mother, there wasn't a lot left to make me a slave

to fashion or even to enable me to take proper precautions against the climate. The game against Hamilton Accies didn't help to improve Jock's mood, either. My display in the first half was enough to bring him down from his seat in the stand on to the touchline to tell me that if I didn't get any better I would be taken off. At least I think he said taken! That match was one of six in succession I was lucky enough to get towards the end of that season, though, and the cumulative good I was able to do myself was, thankfully, enough to give me a future with the club at a time when the failure rate could be cruelly high. My most touching memory is the night a succession of friends came out of Jock Stein's office after being told they were to get free transfers. All ten of them looked thunderstruck and their eyes were full of tears. None of them was able to handle the feeling of devastation sufficiently well to play for another senior club but I was made to appreciate how lucky I had been not to suffer that fate and stunned into realising how hard I would need to work to maintain my place at Celtic Park. It was a lesson I forgot on only one occasion.'

Tommy made his first-team debut for Celtic three weeks before Billy McNeill retired from the game as a player but it would be a further three years, and prompted by the return of his former idol as manager, before he would blossom in a way that came anywhere near his level of personal expectation.

'Billy was someone I watched get out of his car for training each morning and extend his chest to its maximum measurements as he approached the front door as if the air surrounding the park was more bracing than anywhere else.

'When he walked on to the field on a Saturday and did the same thing in front of the captain of the opposing team, there was an impression of consummate authority at work. I had once cleaned his boots each day and when Billy walked into the room I felt there was an aura about him. He would not have been able to return those sentiments since I was one of his first managerial problems when he came back in 1978.

'I was sent off for the first time when I clashed with Colin

Hot shot Burns.

McAdam, whose brother, Tom, was on Celtic's side, in a game against Partick Thistle. I freely admit retaliating by lifting my hands and aiming a blow at Colin's face but the intent was far more serious than the punch, which could only have grazed the chin of someone who was built like Desperate Dan. Colin, though, went down as if he had been felled by a ten-pound hammer. Months later, I was off again during a Skol Cup semi final against Rangers for remarks made to a linesman who had been instrumental in giving a penalty kick against Celtic that could, diplomatically, have been described as controversial. My conversation with him could not have been described as anything other than an indiscreet volley of words which led to the inevitable red card.

'Being the son of a Catholic father and a Protestant mother, I am naturally opposed to bigotry and would deny being the type to have a paranoid suspicion that some refereeing decisions are given specifically to annoy, or even cheat, Celtic. However, in 1979, at Pittodrie, I allowed my emotions to run away with me after Aberdeen had been given a highly questionable free kick that enabled them to take the lead. Soon after, I collided with Gordon Strachan and as the referee went for his red card the irrational thought entered my head that I should take of my jersey and throw it at the match official.

'It was then that the late, great Johnny Doyle gave a demonstration of hands-on management, managing to calm me down by jumping on top of me and managing to make me see sense by telling me that thousands of people had paid good money to go to Aberdeen in order to support Celtic, not to see me discredit the hoops. I was fined £200 by Billy McNeil for that outburst, which was more money than I was getting in wages each week at Celtic Park at that time, and told that I was turning into a liability. At that time, I think the club could have sold me for about £30,000 and nobody would have noticed. The manager told me that with my unpredictable temper and an ankle injury that was causing me to miss an increasing number of games I was of no use to him.

'By then I had won the first of my league championship medals but it was before the semi final of the Scottish Cup the following season that my fragile relationship with the manager came to a head. The place was Seamill, our traditional training camp before such occasions, and the time was the day before our match against Hibs. Billy was introducing his tactical remarks by saying he felt it was ridiculous that he should have to bring in a 35-year-old man, Bobby Lennox, to help put verve and enthusiasm into the side. As he spoke, Billy's eyes scanned the room but when he voiced that particular criticism his eyes met mine and the alarm bells went off inside my head.

'Are you talking about me?' I heard myself say out loud.

"If the cap fits, you'd better wear it, Tommy," Billy replied.

With my voice beginning to tremble with emotion, I couldn't resist saying, 'Well, it doesn't.'

At that point, Billy blew up as well and called for Neilly Mochan, one of Celtic's backroom staff.

Hard work after the sermon from Billy McNeill.

"Neilly, you'd better get him out of here and up the road," Billy said, meaning my residency at our hotel was over and that I was to go home and await my punishment.

'I'd be better off in the house than listening to this ****!' was my last word on the subject. That was when the manager reached the end of his tether and chased me out into the foyer of the hotel, where there was a huge, ornate fireplace. I thought he was going to put me up the chimney because of my insubordination. The gloves were off but that was when Johnny Doyle arrived like the fifth cavalry once again, and once we were separated I was sent to my room convinced that my career at Celtic Park was over. The incident was eventually smoothed over, though, and I played my part in the 5-0 win over Hibs the following day. Come Monday morning, I was on the carpet in Big Billy's office, though, and told a few home truths. I was told, first of all, that I didn't train hard enough to make anything of myself. Then it was pointed out that I gave in to minor injury too easily because I thought I could live off my last good performance for the team. After being called a lazy malingerer of dubious temperament, there aren't a lot of places you can go and I left the manger's office, with its air of the confessional, having apolgised for my conduct and promising to do penance. It was going to the altar six weeks later that really turned my career the right way up, though. When I married Rosemary at St. Francis', in the Gorbals, we set up a home that acted as a haven away from football. But for the wedding contract and Billy McNeill's sermon, I could have drifted away from Celtic without realising what it meant to play for them.'

There then followed what would by ordinary standards be a highly successful period in Tommy's life, the Scottish Cup being won in 1980, League championships in 1981 and 1982 and a league Cup final win in the 1982/3 season which would also turn out to be the last Billy McNeill would spend as manager during his first time at Celtic Park. For Tommy Burns, though, Celtic's problem was that they ignored what was needed most to convert a good side into a great one capable of reviving the club's name where most of the prestige lay, the three major European competitions. Since McNeill retired as a player in 1975, Celtic had lacked a defensive organiser as was constantly evidenced when European ties were lost because of a naive insistence on playing from the heart instead of using the head, when the occasion demanded.

Mixing realism with romaticism was not viewed by Tommy as a desacration of the club's past reputation and their approach. The depression caused by the apparent refusal to see this argument's logic and perennial struggles over money brought about three occasions when Tommy asked Celtic for a transfer.

'I would prefer to say that the pursuit of proper financial reward rather than greed was the root cause because I was the person, don't forget, who once signed a contract with Celtic that involved me getting less money than the one I had agreed to four years earlier. When you ignore the rate of inflation because it's a grand old team to play for, that's when you really have an affection for a club! I always sold myself short at Celtic Park but the quality of life can't be quantified in pounds and pence and if it's true that you can't eat medals, either, then I still derived a lot of nourishment from just looking at mine. There could, and should, have been more, though. My assessment of my own career is that I could have been a better player than I was if I had been surrounded by more quality than we had at Celtic Park. From the time of my first European tie, against Wisla Kracow in the U.E.F.A. Cup of 1976, Celtic reached the quarter final of a European competition only once.

'We went out at the first-round stage seven times, the second round on four occasions and the third round on one other. We didn't even qualify for Europe in 1978. The club seemed to be setting their sights on occasional achievement at a domestic level rather than trying to attain new heights. Arsenal wanted to buy me in 1982 but then, as at other times when I felt restless, a quirk of fate presented itself to prove to me that I was meant to play for Celtic and nobody else. That was still the case when Davie Hay arrived in 1983 to take over a side who had thrown away a nine-point lead in the championship the season before. That should have warned Celtic about a squad that wasn't strong enough, but the top-class players lost weren't replaced and so I asked away once again because of frustration. Chelsea were interested in me but Davie said he could only let me go if Celtic managed to get Frank Gray from Leeds United. That deal fell through, though, and I was asked by the manager if I felt that I could turn myself into a full back. It was the fresh impetus I needed and illustrated that, whenever I was on the verge of leaving Celtic, fate took a hand. After that, I had my best season in years, culminating in the win over St. Mirren at Love Street and that unforgettable day when Celtic won the championship from the side who were supposed to be the favourites, Hearts.

'I said in a radio interview that day that I thanked God for answering my prayers and that was meant as an indication of how badly I wanted the title for Davie Hay, and the supporters. They showed me how much I meant to them on the day in August, 1987, when over forty thousand of them turned out for my testimonial match against Liverpool. It provided me with a memory that was worth one hundred contracts or a million hassles over terms because it was a moving experience to know I had a place in their hearts and a precise standing in Celtic's history.

'When anybody takes on Celtic they take on something unique because it means opposing players, management and supporters who are held together by what I first heard described by Aberdeen's manager, Alex Smith, as the Cause. I have yet to hear the emotional commitment to the club summed up in a more appropriate way. Alex didn't mean the phrase to have any political connotation, only to define the feelings of underdogs bound by a link with the tradition that brought the club into being for humanitarian reasons and made them different from any other. Still being a Celtic supporter, if no longer a player, I can say it is our unity that is our strength. If the day ever dawns when I have to face the prospect of playing against Celtic in a Kilmarnock jersey, I would do so willingly because it would mean I could be back among those fans once again. I will always be Tommy Burns of Celtic, both in the minds of the supporters and my own. That isn't something I have to live with, it's something I wouldn't have

'Playing for Celtic was my pleasure'.

any other way. Whatever disagreements I may have had with them over the years, Celtic owe me absolutely nothing. The pleasure was all mine.'

At the time of his transfer to Kilmarnock, there were suggestions that Tommy had gone into the Second Division rather than confront the team with whom he so closely identifies. This is a misapprehension that can be easily contradicted.

'I did have offers from every Premier League club apart from Aberdeen, Hearts and the obvious one on the South side of Glasgow and I gave them all serious consideration because I knew I could play on for another two years at the highest level. It was not my idea to leave Celtic Park but I had arrived at that stage where I wasn't getting a regular game and I didn't want to lose my sharpness by drifting in and out of the side. I felt I could have done the same type of job for Celtic that Ray Wilkins was doing for Rangers before he went back to London. I could have helped out Paul McStay in the middle of the park and brought experience of what it means to play for Celtic to a team trying to introduce a variety of different players. That wasn't how the club saw my future, though, and I wasn't going to hang about begging for a game.

'The effect on my family was immense when I decided to leave Celtic. I would come home every day and find Rosemary red-eyed, and the scenes at my last game for the club were moving for all of us. The night before we played Ajax, I had agreed to sign for Kilmarnock. When the Fleeting brothers, Jim and Bobby, made their approach, my first reaction was to turn them down. However, it dawned on me that, at the age of 33, I had nothing left to prove to anybody about what I could do at the highest level. Therefore, there could be no possible loss of face involved in going to play in the Second Division. My other consideration had to be that, financially speaking, they did make me the best offer of the lot and I realised I had a responsibility to do what was correct for my wife and children to see us many years into the future and not think about the short term. There has also been an opportunity for me to learn about the game from every side and I have had to encounter what it's like to work with players who haven't known the highest level. All of that will serve me well when I come to look for a job of my own away from Rugby Park. I'm developing my own ideas and work practices and that's why I stopped attending Kilmarnock's reserve game because I didn't want to be used to deliver somebody else's thoughts in the dressing room at half-time. I might as well tell them the story of The Three Bears if the words and ideas are not my own.

'It has been an enjoyable and informative experience otherwise, but I wouldn't patronise any of the people there by saying that anything I achieve will be as sweet as it was when I was a Celtic player. However, it did mean a lot to me when Kilmarnock won promotion to the First Division, even if it was said on television that I looked strange wearing a blue and white scarf during the celebrations after the match. I woud like to think I have sufficient maturity and self-respect to overcome daft prejudices like refusing to pick up, or wear, something in those colours.'

There will be those, and they will not constitute the minority, either, who believe that Celtic Park remains Tommy Burns' rightful place and the location where his learning should be put to use. It is not coincidence that Celtic's most successful times have come when the team has had a nucleus of players who were, essentially, Celtic supporters. It could be, too, that in order to lend a productive hand at the club it is better to have been in another environment for a while. There would be no doubt that Tommy would give of himself with selfless devotion if the opportunity were ever to arise. He knows the depth of the contribution he made to the club as a player and his collection of medals measure his place in Celtic's history.

Tommy Burns' jersey went into the crowd on the day of his testimonial in 1987. His boots were given back to the people two years later on the occasion of his last match. There is also a Paisley businessman who has Tommy Burns' jersey, for which he paid £500. The money was not personal gain but a pre-arranged sum to be donated to Radio Clyde's Cash for Kids appeal which looks after underpriveleged children in the West of Scotland each Christmas. The gesture was made without fuss and was one of a series of similarly unpublicised kindnesses on the part of Tommy Burns, who never loses awareness of his own mortality and can see football in its true perspective, a game but not more important than anything else in life. For what he has achieved in the game, Tommy has always thanked God and gained strength from his deeply-held religious convictions. The time will soon be at hand when guidance and strenth will be sought to sustain him through the next phase of his career, which promises to be as fulfilling as the days when Tommy twisted and Tommy turned on Celtic's behalf.

Tommy Burns   *International Appearances*

1981

May	Northern Ireland (h)	2-0

1982

March	Holland (h)	2-1
May	Wales (h)	1-0
December	Belgium (a)	2-3

1983

May	Northern Ireland (h)	0-0
June	Canada (Toronto)	2-0
June	Canada (Vancouver)	2-0

1988

May	England (a)	0-1

CHAPTER 10

Pat Bonner

PAT BONNER REPRESENTS BOTH THE END OF AN era and an important link in an historical chain that dates back, unbroken, to the last century. The goalkeeper who is now the longest-serving player at Celtic Park was the last person to be signed for the club by the late Jock Stein during his time as manager and also maintains what he would hope will always be the club's association with Ireland, the country of his birth and those who helped found the club. Bonner signed his first agreement with Celtic in a hotel in Letterkenny, watched by his parents and friends from Donegal, where anyone with even a superficial interest in football has a deep affection for Celtic. Before he had ever seen the team play, Pat was fully conversant with their illustrious past and determined to succeed in becoming an integral part of their future. In the years since his name went on the first contract in 1977, Pat has managed to achieve what he set out to do by becoming the goalkeeper with the record number of appearances for Celtic and establishing himself as a symbol for the people from all over Ireland who regularly cross the sea to watch them play. By his performances in the European Championships and the World Cup for the Republic of Ireland, Bonner has also distinguished himself on a broader stage as a typical example of a race used to leaving their homeland in order to earn a living as well as distinction.

Burton Port is a small fishing village near the Republic's border with Northern Ireland and is the place where Pat grew up as one of seven children, five girls and twin boys. When the time came for him to leave his school and home in order to join Celtic, his anxiety over the scale of the change he was about to make was such that Pat can recall having to be confined to bed for a day suffering from the symptoms of nervous strain while family and friends arrived to say goodbye and offer their best wishes.

His much-loved father, who died in 1984, and his mother, who were, coincidentally, married while working in Scotland and had once lived in Copland Road, in the shadow of Ibrox Stadium, were comforted by the fact that their teenage son would divide his time between the houses of a sister each had in Glasgow. However, as the coach that was taking him from his home on the first part of the journey drove through Burton Port, taking him past the places where he had spent the summer holidays from school fishing with his father and brother, Denis, the driver, Anthony Docherty, put on a cassette of Irish music the like of which could bring tears to a pair of contact lenses. The youngster's eyes filled up and his emotions were given full rein. At the same time he made a promise to himself that he would never go back to his parents as the promising player who had failed because he lacked the will to become known as Pat Bonner of Celtic . . . . . .

What the bracing air of Burton Port failed to do was prepare Pat Bonner for the hubbub of city life, particularly in a place like Glasgow with its intense football rivalry and where the idols of supporters have to accept that they are regarded as being partly the property of those who revere them. What his upbringing did give him, however, was a mental fortitude not always typical of the members of his profession.

'To this day, I am perfectly happy with my own company, at ease with myself wherever I am with Celtic or the Republic of Ireland. It means I can drive my car into the countryside,

A lifetime's ambition — Bonner of Celtic.

leave it and go for long walks on my own that give me time to gather and think my thoughts. It helps me deal with the pressures of being with a big club. Football has given me a lifestyle and taken me to places I could otherwise never have dreamed of if I had stayed at home, and for that I am duly grateful, but it all requires an element of self-sacrifice as well.'

It was the 1970 World Cup finals, staged in Mexico and won by Brazil, that inspired the young Bonner when his parents allowed him to stay up late and watch every match. It was a near neighbour, Dom O'Donnell, who was the most ardent football fan in Burton Port, and visitors to his home were made fully aware of where his particular allegiance lay before they had finished wiping their feet at the doorway. A huge photograph of Celtic's European Cup-winning side of 1967 adorned his hallway, and though no Scottish matches were shown on Irish television, Pat learned to name those eleven Scotsmen on sight. A natural athlete, the schoolboy who played for the local amateur side, Keadue Rovers, had

planned, on completion of his exams, to go to Belfast
Polytechnic to study as a physical education instructor.

'Before I could follow that road, though, I was picked to
represent Ulster in an inter-county match in Dublin, There
were, and obviously still are, so many Celtic supporters in
Donegal that I still do not know to this day who tipped off
Sean Fallon about that game, but the man who was then Jock
Stein's assistant manager watched me play and introduced
himself afterwards. Whoever the informant was, I would like
to thank him but there are dozens who take the credit! The idea
of being invited to play a trial for Celtic was, for me,
overwhelming, but the circumstances under which I got a game
were not exactly what I expected. I went to Glasgow with my
father for company, but it was the start of a severe winter and
the only game I could get was as a trialist with Coltness Juniors
against East Kilbride Thistle. I was down on the team sheet as
Newman and when the referee came into the dressing room and
asked what my first name was a voice quicker than mine said,
"Paul".

'After that, the waiting was the worst part. I went back to
Burton Port and Keadue Rovers but then, one night, our
manager, Manus McCole, came to me and said Sean Fallon
had telephoned to ask if I could play for Celtic in a youth
tournament that was to be held in France.'

The event is best remembered by Pat for reasons that have
nothing to do with the way he played, which he felt had been
not particularly well, but all to do with his being an innocent
abroad. Before the start of his first game, the national anthem
of the competing countries was played as the sides were lined
up on the pitch. Those who were from Great Britain stood to
attention for 'God Save The Queen', except for Celtic's goalkeeper. He broke away from the rest and had to be brought
back and told about his diplomatic *faux pas*. Being from the
particular part of the world Pat came from, he had never heard
the tune before!

'One of Celtic's coaching staff on that trip was Frank

'But for Frank O'Connor,
I wonder how my life would
have turned out.'

Connor and, but for his presence, I sometimes wonder how my
life would have turned out. As well as being a tremendous
enthusiast, Frank was also a former Celtic goalkeeper and he
was able to peer through the inexperience and the basic flaws
and spot the raw potential that could be turned into something
of a higher standard. That turned out to be the luck of the Irish
in my case. The other thing Frank did was to take away the last
vestige of boyhood in me by insisting I get my shoulder-length

hair cut before I could call myself a proper Celtic man. That transformation took place in an old fashioned Glasgow barber shop before we left for France. My uncle, whose house I was staying in, tried to take me to one of the trendier salons in Glasgow but they all worked on a booking system and I had no time to wait, so he took me to the place he used. By the time the barber had finished with me, I had slicked down hair that was parted in a middle shed. I looked more like a player out of the early photographs of the team that were unearthed during Celtic's Centenary year. Frank thought it was smart, though!'

When it came time for Pat to return to Glasgow on a full-time basis, Jock Stein and Sean Fallon had gone from the club to be replaced by Billy McNeill and John Clark. Fallon had been chauffeur and confidant as well as compatriot and it was at that point the independent streak in the young Irishman had to sustain him against the pitfalls of being in a strange city without friends of his own.

'It was so quiet where I came from that you only spoke to people you knew well and waited for the other person to speak first if they were strangers. I was determined, though, that I wouldn't allow anything to upset me and take every setback that came my way as a spur to do even better. I had heard various stories in the dressing room that stiffened my resolve as I absorbed Celtic's history at first hand. For example, one of my predecessors from the Republic of Ireland, another goal-keeper called Tom Lally, had found it so hard to settle in Glasgow he had spent every afternoon of his life in one cinema or another to fend off boredom and homesickness. On a more serious level, I had also been told the story of Ally Hunter, a Scotland internationalist, who had been badly affected because of a bad goal he had lost in a World Cup qualifying tie against Czechoslovakia, even though the game was won and his side made it to the finals in West Germany. Apparently, Ally had never been quite the same goalkeeper for Celtic after that. I found that hard to understand and I speak as someone who, in his first season, lost seven goals to Rangers in a reserve match

When Irish eyes are smiling.

at Celtic Park. Drawing a direct comparison between a World Cup tie and something like that might seem illogical to some but, for committed supporters, losing that precise number to that team in particular is a serious business. I remember John Clark consoling me in the dressing room afterwards by saying that Rangers' team had been far more experienced than ours and that I had been let down by some of the players in front of me, but I was in no danger of running home to Ireland with my world shattered around me, in any case.

'A goalkeeper simply can't afford to be a withdrawn character, as television film of me during Celtic's matches tends to prove. It is a vital part of my job to organise the players in front of me from the forwards back to the defenders and that is why it makes me laugh when I have people say to me after the team has won convincingly that I had nothing to do. Making sure the other players maintain their concentration for all of the ninety minutes is, I can assure you, far more exhausting than the physical exertion of hurling myself around to save the ball.'

It is the case that younger Celtic supporters tend to be less tolerant of any mishaps which come the way of the team because, throughout the modern era, they have been allowed to luxuriate in success on an extravagant scale at regular intervals. Their forebears, who can, for example, readily recall the eight years that passed without a trophy being won from the time of the League Cup final win over Rangers in 1957 until the Scottish Cup was won in 1965 know from experience that real life is not like that. Bonner's position as the elder statesman in today's Celtic side has also enabled him to take a more mature and considered view of what goes on around him at the only senior club he has played for, such as the preoccupation with the Lisbon Lions and the comparisons that are constantly made between players of that era and all of those who have come after them.

'I know that every Celtic goalkeeper has been measured against Ronnie Simpson since he retired in 1970, and probably unfavourable conclusions have been arrived at over the years as well. I am not going to enter into the debate on my own behalf beyond saying that I will let my record speak for itself. It would be my contention that I have proved myself capable of doing what any other goalkeeper in Britain can do and, at the same time, dismissed the notion that there is something fundamentally wrong with goalkeepers who earn their living in the Premier League. Having played in the top ten for all of my professional life, I have to be considered Scottish in that

Lending a hand — Dispelling a myth.

respect and it used to annoy me intensely when I was overlooked by the manger of my own national team at one point for what I can only suspect was distrust.

'People like Jimmy Greaves have made a career out of criticising Scottish goalkeepers on television and Eoin Hand, when he had the job as the Republic of Ireland's manager, never once came to see me play for Celtic in a domestic match while putting players from the lower leagues in England ahead of me for the national side. The only time I can remember Eoin Hand watching me play was against Ajax in Amsterdam on the night when we put Johan Cruyff and his team-mates in their

place in the European Cup. That struck me as being unfair but
I like to think that since Jack Charlton took over the job I have
established myself and proved to everyone in the Republic that,
whatever they have been brainwashed into believing about
goalkeepers in Scotland, it is mythology. It also means a lot to
me to be fully accepted by the people of my own country. My
only regret in football is that my father, Andrew, was not
spared long enough to see me help the Republic qualify for the
European Championships and then the World Cup finals for
the first time, but I like to think he's looking over me and
feeling proud just the same.'

It was, fittingly, on St. Patrick's Day, 1979 that Pat made
his first-team debut for Celtic, against Motherwell, in a game
won by two Bobby Lennox goals. Two weeks later, as part of a
series of re-arranged fixtures caused by the disruption of winter
that was ultimately to help Celtic come from behind and win
the Premier Division championship in the last league game of
the season, Pat played against Motherwell again, this time at
Fir Park. He would rather draw a discreet veil over his
performance on that occasion, in spite of the fact that Celtic
won by the odd goal in seven. At the start of the season that
followed, Peter Latchford, the Englishman who was exceptionally popular with the supporters after his transfer from West
Bromwich Albion, was to break a bone in his hand on the day
before the testimonial match for Celtic's captain, Danny
McGrain, against Manchester United. If goalkeepers are the
only people actually given the opportunity to literally grab a
chance with both hands, Pat was not going to be the one to let
that moment pass.

An outstanding display in that match then led to the
remarkably consistent accomplishment of playing 169
consecutive matches at fully competitive level from August,
1980 until October, 1983 and making the position his own.

'It is probably the case that Scotland is the only country
where that kind of thing could happen and for that, and the
understanding of Billy McNeill during his first time in charge

Goalkeepers have to be two people.

of the team, I have to be thankful. I had once been on trial with Leicester City as a schoolboy and I know from that experience that I would not have been given the same latitude in England. Billy can be an abrasive man with players and might not always be the most patient of individuals when they try to express themselves but he was willing to let me learn by my mistakes, and they must have been plentiful, in the first team. It was during that time I had to come out of my shell and settle into a team that was confident enough to win championships. Goalkeepers have to be domineering by nature because the penalty for not being that way can be severe. If I introduce the case of Ian Andrews at this point it is only to make a point about how players have to be two personalities in one. Ian came to Celtic while I was badly injured, something that can be gone into in greater detail later on, but found his career with the club over before it had properly begun and had eventually to move on to Southampton without making any more than a brief series of appearances, even though he had cost £300,000.

'It was not just the fact that Ian had the misfortune to lose a handful of goals to Rangers at Ibrox that prevented him from making an impact but his general demeanour as well. Ian had a polite, well-mannered way with him and a goalkeeper, unfortunately, can't afford to be that way. The irony of my situation with Celtic was that, in spite of having a steady rise to prominence in a successful side, it took Billy McNeill's departure for Manchester City and the subsequent appointment of David Hay at that difficult juncture to really allow me the space to develop.

'The ups and downs of Davie's time as manager have been analysed thoroughly since he lost his job at Celtic Park in 1987 and need little by way of further dissection from me but I have felt since that if he had known then what he knows now about a job of that magnitude he would have been all the better for it. All I can say is he did me a favour and would un-doubtedly make a good manager for some other club today, and none of this has anything to do with the fact that Davie once called me the best goalkeeper in Britain. To summarise those four years he had in control, during which we won the Scottish Cup and the league title in successive seasóns, Davie improved me to the extent that, by the time he left, I felt confident enough in myself to believe that I could save absolutely anything that came my way.'

The dramatic sequence of events which saw Celtic indulge in the unusual practice of dismissing Hay and re-employ McNeill coincided with the advent of the club's centenary season in May, 1987. There are those who believe that what followed over the next twelve months had as much to do with what McNeill calls the 'fairytale aspect' which attaches itself to Celtic as much as anything else. Bonner would be able to point to the statistics of the team's championship-winning effort, however, as proof of something more tangible at work. In 36 league games, only 24 goals were lost, a record for the Premier League and something that does not come about by chance. If someone had been watching over the goalkeeper, in fact, He must have been guilty of deserting His post during the climatic phase of that season because Pat was then afflicted by the injury problem that would cause him genuine doubts over his

Celtic in safe hands.

future. A typically breathtaking run towards the Cup Final that would complete the first 'double' won by the club in 11 years was interrupted for Pat in the week of the last match of the season, against Dundee United at Hampden.

'It started with a nagging pain in the small of my back that would affect me as soon as I woke up in the morning but relented as the day wore on after exercising. It got to the stage, though, where, if I was out for a meal with my wife, Anne, I could only sit for ten minutes without experiencing discomfort and then I would have to get up and walk about the restaurant to get some relief. Various medical tests were done on me, including one to see if I had developed arthritis, and the whole episode began to make me feel irritable. On the Tuesday before the Cup Final, I woke up with a shooting pain running down my leg but with the help of manipulation from Celtic's physiotherapist, Brian Scott, I was able to go with the rest of the squad to Seamill two days later to start preparing for the match.

'Supporters who avidly follow everything to do with the team are used to reading about players having fitness tests and might sometimes wonder if such a thing really does go on or how stringent and decisive they can be. I can assure you I was put through one of those examinations at Seamill and was so desperate to play in the Cup Final I was straining every muscle to prove I could play my part to the full at Hampden. The player involved is always the first to know exactly how fit he is and, much as I might have been reluctant to admit it, I had to own up to myself that my leg had been deadened by the pain. The spring I needed to get from that area in order to do my job properly had gone and under those circumstances there was no other option but to concede that playing in such a vital game was out of the question. I don't mind admitting, either, that after the knowing looks had been exchanged by the management, I slumped against a wall outside the team's hotel and slid to the ground crying like a little boy. Not playing in that game was the biggest disappointment in my career at Celtic Park.'

With the aid of yet more manipulative treatment from the Republic of Ireland's physiotherapist, Mick Byrne, Pat was able to recover sufficiently to go with his country to the European Championships in West Germany. But for a late and fortuitous goal lost to Holland, he might have helped them qualify for the latter stages as well, though Bonner and the rest were able to return to their respective clubs with honour fully intact. However, the goalkeeper's injury worries were only just starting. Entry into a private hospital in Glasgow was followed by an immediate operation on his back and then the anxiety of waiting to see how successful the surgery had been. In the interim, Celtic bought Ian Andrews from Leicester City for £300,000, prompting understandable speculation that Pat Bonner's problem was far more serious than anyone cared to think.

'At the time, I had to make positive-sounding noises in public and say that I had no fears for my future but, inwardly, I knew that might not be entirely accurate. I couldn't blame Celtic for taking steps to cover themselves, though, because

Billy McNeill knew I was going to miss the first three months of the season at least as a result of the normal, convalescent process. The manager had experienced a similar problem at Maine Road when Manchester City's goalkeeper Alex Williams, had suffered the same injury and, tragically, had never made a full recovery. Lots of thoughts had gone through my mind about the future, not all of them encouraging, but then the Irish in me took over. Where I come from, people are used to making their living the hard way. My father had gone into house building after he stopped going to sea for the fishing and worked long hours for small wages to support his family. In the end, he worked himself to death but I was still determined not to let my career just slip away from me for the want of trying.'

It would be gratuitously glib to say that the rest is history. Determination and bravery had their own reward when the Scottish Cup winners medal that had eluded Pat the season before was eventually given to him for being part of the side who salvaged the one that came after by defeating Rangers at Hampden.

Once again the misfortunes that, from youth, he had resolved would only be inspirational stepping stones on the way to something better had been overcome to reinforce his own philosophy on the game and its vagaries.

'If I came to Scotland with a lot to learn about Celtic's traditions, the first and most lasting impression I formed is that there has to be an imperishable spirit about every player at this club. The team's history tells us this has always been the case because Celtic do not accept defeat and have frequently hurdled supposedly impossible obstacles to win trophies. In my time, there have been examples of players whose temperament made them a part of the club's fabric, Danny McGrain, Tommy Burns and Roy Aiken being some of them. Their affection for Celtic did not diminish when they left Celtic Park, either. There was, for example, the day of an Old Firm Scottish Cup-tie when Celtic had to win at home or accept the season was over months ahead of its time. We were staying at Seamill to concentrate our minds on achieving that result when, on the morning of the game, I got a telephone call to my room. It was Roy Aitken and another former Celtic player, Mark McGhee, who were motoring from their new homes in Newcastle to watch the match and were using the telephone in Mark's car. As well as passing on their best wishes and offering words of encouragement, Roy and Mark were full of confidence over Celtic's ability not to fail when it mattered most. It has to be that way if Celtic are to succeed and that call was the start of a day that proved a lot to me. The composition of the side had changed dramatically, with Polish and English players arriving at Celtic Park. It was all right for the Irish because they had the historical affinity with the club but I wondered if the rest could ever become filled with the same spirit. The defeat of Rangers removed any shadow of doubt that they had indeed absorbed the lesson that Celtic is not just a football team but a special atmosphere they must strive to help maintain and prosper.'

Being the longest-serving player at Celtic Park has also given Pat the experience to know that undiluted success is not possible and that pre-eminence goes in cycles. There is, therefore, much for him still to achieve with the club, and it is his intention to stay with Celtic until his career finally ends.

'I have honestly never felt the urge to play for anybody else. Celtic fulfil me on every level, all the more so now that my international career is progressing satisfactorily at the same time. I have a domestic lifestyle that I am greatly contented with having my wife Anne, and my two children, Andrew and Melissa Anne. It is my hope one day to build a home in Burton Port for all of us but I do retain a strong sense of my Irish identity in Glasgow because of the regular visits to Celtic Park made by so many of my countrymen. I think it is necessary to be happy in this life and all I can hope for is Celtic recognising the service I have given to them. If they look after me properly, then I have no wish to go elsewhere and look forward to many more years at the peak of my powers. When the time comes, I

Bonner — the link in an historical chain.

will then think about getting up a business that might allow me to divide my time between Scotland and Ireland.'

Fate carried one of the Bonner twins to Scotland, while taking the other, Dennis, to America and then home again to play for Sligo Rovers. It is said that whenever their games are televised Dennis' name is always prefixed by a mention of him being the brother of Celtic's Pat Bonner. Their mother, Grace, and sisters, Margaret, Mamie, Anne, Cathy and Bridget Mary, as well as thousands more well wishers all over Ireland and Scotland, would surely not take umbrage at that. Pat is, after all, a link in the historical chain between two countries brought about by a football team, and the fact that it is particularly safe in that pair of hands is no small achievement or limited cause for satisfaction.

Pat Bonner   *International Appearances*

1981

May	Poland (a)	0-3

1982

April	Algeria (a)	0-2

1983

November	Malta (h)	8-0

1984

April	Israel (a)	0-3
June	China (a)	1-0

1985

February	Italy (h)	1-2
February	Israel (a)	0-0
March	England (a)	0-2
May	Norway (h)	0-0

1986

April	Uruguay (h)	1-1
May	Iceland (a)	2-1
September	Belgium (a)	2-2
October	Scotland (h)	0-0
November	Poland (a)	0-1

1987

February	Scotland (h)	1-0
April	Bulgaria (a)	1-2
April	Belgium (h)	0-0
May	Brazil (h)	1-0
May	Luxembourg (a)	2-0
October	Bulgaria (h)	2-0

1988

March	Rumania (h)	2-0
April	Yugoslavia (h)	2-0
June	Norway (a)	0-0
May	England (a)	1-0
June	U.S.S.R. (a)	1-1
June	Holland (a)	0-1
November	Spain (a)	0-2

1989

February	France (h)	0-0
February	Hungary (a)	0-0
April	Spain (h)	1-0
May	Malta (h)	2-0
June	Hungary (h)	2-0
September	West Germany (h)	1-1
October	Northern Ireland (h)	3-0
November	Malta (h)	2-0

1990

March	Wales (h)	1-0
May	Finland (h)	1-1
June	England (a)	1-1
June	Egypt (a)	0-0
June	Holland (a)	1-1
June	Rumania (a)	0-0
		(Eire win on penalties)
June	Italy (a)	0-1